UNCROWNED BUT NOT
UNSHAKEN
The Legacy of Queen Vashti

UNCROWNED BUT NOT UNSHAKEN

The Legacy of Queen Vashti

DR. NORA SHARIFF-BORDEN

Contents

A Note From the Author

Dear Reader,

Thank you for purchasing this book and joining me on a journey through the story of Queen Vashti. It is my heartfelt prayer that as you walk through these pages, you will not only learn more about this remarkable woman but also reflect on the powerful lessons her story offers for our own lives today.

Queen Vashti's story has deeply inspired and enlightened me in ways I never expected. Her strength, her dignity, and her courage to stand for what was right even when it meant losing everything has left an indelible mark on my heart. Through her quiet defiance, I was reminded that God truly does have a divine plan for each and every one of us. Even when we cannot see the full picture, or when His plans don't align with our expectations, we must trust that His ways are higher, and His timing is perfect.

Jeremiah 29:11 tells us, *"For I know the plans I have for you,"* *declares the Lord, "plans to prosper you and not to harm you,*

"I Was Born To Be A Queen"

plans to give you hope and a future." I hold tightly to this promise and believe that, at some point, Queen Vashti recognized the greater plan that God had for the Jewish people. I believe she was willing to sacrifice her royal position in order to play her role in unfolding His divine will.

Sometimes, we are called to surrender what looks good or feels comfortable in order to step into something far greater. This book is more than a historical or biblical account it's a call to examine our own willingness to obey God, even when it costs us something.

As you read and reflect on Queen Vashti's decision, I encourage you to ask yourself: *What would you do if you were in her shoes? Would you have had the strength to trust in God's greater plan?*

May this book be a source of inspiration, strength, and transformation in your life. May Queen Vashti's story awakens something within you a call to courage, a call to purpose, and a call to walk boldly in the path that God has set before you.

Blessings always,
Dr. Nora Shariff-Borden

"I Was Born To Be A Queen"

Acknowledgments

First and foremost, I give all glory and thanks to You, Lord for filling my heart with the words to write this powerful book, *on Queen Vashti* Thank You for revealing the incredible power You have placed within me the power to walk in greatness in all that I do. The importance of always standing up for what is right!

To my incredible husband,

Your unwavering support in everything I do means more to me than words can ever fully express. Whether I am chasing a dream, walking through a challenge, or simply navigating the day-to-day, you are always right there by my side, steadfast, loyal, and full of love. Your presence in my life is a gift I treasure deeply. Thank you for loving me unconditionally for seeing me at my best and at my worst, thank you for never wavering in your commitment to me. You embody the kind of love that is patient, kind, and enduring, and for that, I am eternally grateful.

"I Was Born To Be A Queen"

"Uncrowned But Not Unshaken: The Legacy of Queen Vashti"

Proverbs 18:22 says, *"He who finds a wife finds what is good and receives favor from the LORD."* My love, you have truly found a good thing. But just as importantly, I have found an extraordinary blessing in you. You are God's perfect match for me my soul mate, my protector, my confidant, and my greatest encourager.

Every day I thank God for choosing you for me. Through every season of life, you have proven to be the man I can count on, lean on, and dream with. You reflect God's favor in my life, and I will never take that for granted.

I love you beyond words, deeper than any ocean, and more powerfully than any expression could convey. Thank you for being you. Thank you for being mine. Forever and always, I am yours.

To my beloved mother, thank you for always believing in me and my visions. You were the epitome of greatness strong, determined, and full of wisdom. You instilled in me the value of hard work and perseverance, and for that, I am forever grateful. I love and miss you deeply. How I wish you were here to witness the fruits of your unwavering love and support. Your guidance has shaped me into the successful businesswoman I am today. You raised four powerful, God-fearing daughters, and your legacy of faith and resilience lives on in us. You were truly one of a kind mother.

"I Was Born To Be A Queen"

"Uncrowned But Not Unshaken:
The Legacy of Queen Vashti"

To my beautiful sisters, thank you for your unwavering love, encouragement, and support. Your presence in my life is a true blessing.

To my wonderful children, my greatest desire as your mother is to lead by example, walking in faith and purpose. I am so proud of each of you. I thank God every day for choosing me to be your mother.

To my precious grandchildren, you are my inspiration. I love you with the love of Christ, and I pray that you always remember—through Him, *all things are possible.*

To my extraordinary and powerful pastor, the Reverend Dr. Cynthia L. Hale, thank you for being a beacon of strength and perseverance. You have shattered barriers and silenced the mouths of doubter's proving that God qualifies those He calls. Your confidence in God's vision has been a profound lesson for me. Thank you for teaching us that with faith, dedication, and a willingness to pay the price for our dreams, *anything* is possible.

With a heart full of gratitude, I honor each of you who has played a part in my journey. May God bless you abundantly.

"I Was Born To Be A Queen"

"Uncrowned But Not Unshaken:
The Legacy of Queen Vashti"

To My Dear Friend Michelle McKinney Hammond,

I want to extend my deepest gratitude for being such a remarkable source of inspiration in my life. Your wisdom, insight, and unwavering encouragement played a power full role in igniting the passion behind this book on Queen Vashti. Our heartfelt discussion about this courageous and dignified Queen opened my eyes to layers of her story that I had never seen before. You helped me see Queen Vashti not just as a historical figure, but as a symbol of strength, identity, and divine purpose.

Your ability to bring biblical characters to life with grace and boldness has always inspired me, and I consider you one of the most gifted authors I know. Your own body of work reflects a deep understanding of God's heart for women, and your voice has served as both a guide and a catalyst for my own writing journey.

Thank you Michelle, for helping me see the deeper truths in Queen Vashti story, for encouraging me to pursue this book, and for believing in my voice. I pray that the same spirit of truth, boldness, and purpose that you carry continues to flow through every word of this project. You are truly a treasure, and I am blessed to call you my sister in Christ and my Friend.

Blessings Always
Dr. Nora Shariff-Borden

"I Was Born To Be A Queen"

Preface

This powerful book about Queen Vashti is a must-read for every woman seeking courage, purpose, and clarity in moments of challenge. It sheds light on the often-overlooked story of a queen whose bold stance changed the course of history not through loud proclamations, but through quiet defiance that echoed across generations. Queen Vashti's actions spoke louder than any words, showing us, that dignity, self-respect, and inner strength are sometimes best expressed through the decisions we make when no one else is willing to take a stand.

In a time when obedience was expected without question, Queen Vashti refused to compromise her values. She stood her ground, fully aware of the consequences, and in doing so, became a symbol of integrity, self-worth, and divine purpose. Her story reminds us that doing what is right may not always be popular, but it is always powerful.

This book is more than a historical account—it's a timely call to action for every woman who has ever doubted her voice, second-guessed her worth, or feared the cost of say-

"I Was Born To Be A Queen"

ing "no" when it mattered most. It will challenge you to examine your own convictions and help you embrace the beauty of taking risks when they are necessary for your growth and your truth.

As you embark on this journey through the life and legacy of Queen Vashti, I invite you to open your heart, release the weight of fear and uncertainty, and step into the awareness that you are chosen for something extraordinary. May this book inspire you to stand boldly, love deeply, and walk confidently in your God-given identity even when the world expects otherwise. Let Queen Vashti's courageous stand awakens the queen within you.

"I Was Born To Be A Queen"

Nora Shariff-Borden

Dr. Nora Shariff-Borden and her three younger sisters were born and raised in Boston, Massachusetts. Nora and her husband, Neil, live outside Atlanta, Georgia. Together they have six adult children, 14 grandchildren, and four great-grandchildren. The seed of Christianity was planted in her life by her Grandmother, Nora Dunn.

Dr. Nora moved away from the Lord and became a Muslim. Once she woke up and realized an emptiness that was in her spirit, and that she missed her Lord and Savior, Jesus Christ. God saw fit to bring her back to Him over 30 years ago, and she accepted her call from God to become a Christian inspirational speaker.

Dr. Nora founded Business Women On The Move For God (BWOTMFG). This organization inspires and encourages God's people to be who He has called them to be, which is awesome, powerful, mighty, and great. God wants them to be clear about their goals and dreams and how to achieve them through Him. Dr. Nora started BWOTMFG because she loves seeing people own their

"I Was Born To Be A Queen"

greatness and learn how to walk in it daily! She wants the next generation of young people to realize their greatness and be unapologetic about it. Dr. Nora wants people to be able to get up when they have fallen and to learn the importance of continuing their journey! She wants them to be bold about their relationship with their Lord Jesus Christ.

Dr. Nora is the Founder and CEO of Spiritual Touch TV, where she hosts an online show, Real Conversations with Nora, which focuses on the many issues that people face every day through transparent conversations. Dr. Nora digs deep to help people deal with their issues and to help them reclaim their authentic selves and overcome their obstacles so, they can navigate through life successfully.

Dr. Nora believes she has a gift from God that allows her to connect with God's people. She believes that if you can touch the heart of people, they will do all they can to support you. Dr. Nora's goal is to teach people that their words have the power to change their lives. She also believes she can help them paint a picture of what they want their life to look like so that when it appears, all they have to do is step into it.

Dr. Nora is a woman with a serious mission who believes that if she meets the true needs of God's people with total sincerity and commitment to serve as God has called her to do, her work will not be in vain.

In March of 2022, Nora was bestowed an Honorary Doctorate Degree from Trinity International University of Ambassadors (TIUA).

On December 3rd of, 2022, she received the Presidential Lifetime Achievement Award, Also, in February of 2023, in honor of Black History Month Dr. Nora was awarded The Presidential Legacy Lifetime Achievement Award from Trinity International University of Ambassadors, in honor of our 44th President, Barack Obama. June of 2023, she was awarded The International Anthology of the Year Award by TIUA School of Business for Your Faith Will Make You Unstoppable.

On June 12th, 2024, She *was presented with A Resolution Honoring From Representative Billy Mitchell and Dr. Jacqueline Mohair, Found of Trinity International University of Ambassadors at Georgia State Capital! This honor was presented to her for being selected to serve as a United Nations Peace Ambassador to the United Nations in New York!*

Her future projects for BWOTMFG include developing a program called Teen Tv Media and establishing a $10,000 scholarship program for young People who major in business.

"I Was Born To Be A Queen"

I Am Queen Vashti

Queen Vashti Introduction:

I am Queen Vashti, as a woman I faced some challenging and pivotal situations during my time as queen. You see my husband the King of Persia held a grand feast and, in a moment of revelry, commanded me Queen Vashti to appear before him and his guests to display my beauty to his drunk friends. As a woman with great character, I refused the king's command, a decision that had significant consequences. As a leader sometimes we have to make decisions that are right before God and not man, which comes with great consequences.

Vashti's Decision:

Refusal to Comply:

My Dignity and Self-Respect was more important to me than pleasing the King. I believe that my refusal is often interpreted as a stand for dignity and self-respect. I chose

"I Was Born To Be A Queen"

not to be objectified or humiliated by appearing before the king and his intoxicated guests.

Courage: This is where my integrity and courage stepped in! I believe that God had a greater plan for my life and for the lives of His people.

Although I was Deposed of as Queen, I believe it showed the other women what it means to have courage, respect integrity before our great God.

Replacement: Queen Vashti's removal set the stage for Esther, a Jewish woman, to become queen. This change from Queen Vashti to Queen Esther had a significant implications for the Jewish people, as Queen Esther later played a crucial role in saving them from a planned massacre.

Interpretations and Legacy:

They say I am a Feminist Icon:

I am often seen as a pro-to-feminist figure who stood up against male authority and the objectification of women. My actions as a leader and a servant of God is celebrated by many as an early assertion of women's rights.

"I Was Born To Be A Queen"

"Uncrowned But Not Unshaken:
The Legacy of Queen Vashti"

Symbol of Resistance:

I believe I embody the spirit of resistance against unjust demands and the courage to accept the consequences of standing firm on one's principles. That is the mark of true leadership not only for myself but also for those who follow me now and in the future. My actions paved the way for another remarkable woman and leader, Queen Esther.

In summary: I Queen Vashti handled my situation with a firm stand for my dignity despite the risks involved. My story continues to resonate as a powerful example of what a true leader does for herself and those, she has been chosen to lead.

I Am Queen Vashti A Powerful Leader
IN My Times And The Future.

"I Was Born To Be A Queen"

Queen Vashti's History Information

Although the bible doesn't give much information on Queen Vashti's birth place. It is suggested that she descended from the Babylonian royal line possibly as the daughter of Belshazzar and granddaughter of Nebuchadnezzar before being taken captive and later becoming Persian.

The Bible does not name Queen Vashti's parents. However, Jewish rabbinic tradition (Midrash) offers an interpretation about her lineage:

► **According to the Midrash (Jewish commentary):**

Queen Vashti is believed to be the daughter of King Belshazzar, the last king of Babylon.

This would make her the granddaughter of King Nebuchadnezzar, who is famously known in the Bible for the destruction of Jerusalem and the Babylonian exile.

This tradition suggests that after the Persian conquest of Babylon, Queen Vashti known as Babylonian royalty —

was taken into the Persian court and eventually married to King Ahasuerus (Xerxes I) as part of a political alliance or spoil of war.

▶ Summary:

These details are not historical facts but are based on theological tradition and Jewish oral history, aiming to give context and moral lessons through narrative symbolism.

Although the Bible does not specify Queen Vashti's age when she became queen, and there are no historical records that provide her exact age either.

However, based on cultural context and rabbinic tradition, we can make an educated estimate:

◈ Historical and Cultural Context:

In ancient Persia, royal marriages often took place when young women were in their mid to late teens, sometimes even earlier.

Queen Vashti was already queen at the time of the great banquet in Esther 1, which took place in the third year of King Ahasuerus's reign (Xerxes I, historically around 483 B.C.).

"I Was Born To Be A Queen"

◈ **Conclusion:**

◈ **Estimated age:** Of Queen Vashti was likely in her mid to late teens, possibly around 15 to 18 years old when she became queen — but this is not confirmed in scripture or history.

The Babylonian people were part of an ancient Mesopotamian civilization located in what is now modern-day Iraq. They were a Semitic people, closely related to the Akkadians, Assyrians, and later, the Arameans and Hebrews. Because of their geographic location and ethnic roots, their skin color can be understood based on historical, archaeological, and genetic studies.

The Babylonians most likely had olive to medium brown skin, dark hair, and dark eyes — resembling modern Middle Eastern people. Babylon was ethnically diverse, so some variation in appearance was likely. I believe she had beautiful Olive Brown Skin.

"I Was Born To Be A Queen"

The Order Of The King

Esther 1 (NIV)

1. This is what happened during the time of Xerxes, the Xerxes who ruled over 127 provinces stretching from India to Cush:

2. At that time King Xerxes reigned from his royal throne in the citadel of Susa,

3. And in the third year of his reign, he gave a banquet for all his nobles and officials. The military leaders of Persia and Media, the princes, and the nobles of the provinces were present.

4. For a full 180 days he displayed the vast wealth of his kingdom and the splendor and glory of his majesty.

5. When these days were over, the king gave a banquet, lasting seven days, in the enclosed garden of the king's Palace for all the people from the least to the greatest, who were in the citadel of Susa.

"I Was Born To Be A Queen"

6. The garden had hangings of white and blue linen, fastened with cords of white linen and purple material to silver rings on marble pillars. There were couches of gold and silver on a mosaic pavement of porphyry, marble, mother-of-pearl and other costly stones.

7. Wine was served in goblets of gold, each one different from the other, and the royal wine was abundant, in keeping with the king's liberality.

8. By the king's command each guest was allowed to drink in his own way, for the king instructed all the wine stewards to serve each man what he wished.

9. Queen Vashti also gave a banquet for the women in the royal palace of King Xerxes.

10. On the seventh day, when King Xerxes was in high spirits from wine, he commanded the seven eunuchs who served him Mehuman, Biztha, Harbona, Bigtha, Abagtha, Zethar and Karkas—

11. To bring before him Queen Vashti, wearing her royal crown, in order to display her beauty to the people and nobles, for she was lovely to look at.

12. But when the attendants delivered the king's command, Queen Vashti refused to come. Then the king became furious and burned with anger.

"I Was Born To Be A Queen"

13. Since it was customary for the king to consult experts in matters of law and justice, he spoke with the wise men who understood the times.

14. And were closest to the king Karshena, Shethar, Admatha, Tarshish, Meres, Marsena and Memukan, the seven nobles of Persia and Media who had special access to the king and were highest in the kingdom.

15. "According to law, what must be done to Queen Vashti," he asked, "because she has not obeyed the command of King Xerxes that the eunuchs have taken to her?"

16. Then Memukan replied in the presence of the king and the nobles, "Queen Vashti has done wrong, not only against the king but also against all the nobles and the peoples of all the provinces of King Xerxes.

17. For the queen's conduct will become known to all the women, and so they will despise their husbands and say, King Xeres commanded Queen Vashti to be brought before him, but she would not come.'

18. This very day the Persian and Median women of the nobility who have heard about the queen's conduct will respond to all the king's nobles in the same way. There will be no end of disrespect and discord.

"I Was Born To Be A Queen"

19. "Therefore, if it pleases the king, let him issue a royal decree and let it be written in the laws of Persia and Media, which cannot be repealed, that Queen Vashti is never again to enter the presence of King Xerxes. Also let the king give her royal position to someone else who is better than she.

20. Then when the king's edict is proclaimed throughout all his vast realm, all the women will respect their husbands, from the least to the greatest."

21. The king and his nobles were pleased with this advice, so the king did as Memukan proposed.

22. He sent dispatches to all parts of the kingdom, to each province in its own script and to each people in their own language, proclaiming that every man should be ruler over his own household, using his native tongue.

Looking Beyond the Throne: King Xerxes, Queen Vashti and God's Greater Plan

Even though King Xerxes held the ultimate authority to make decisions regarding his kingdom including the fate of Queen Vashti I couldn't help but reflect on how much he relied on the opinions of those around him. As a ruler, it's understandable to seek wise counsel, especially when public image and political influence are at stake.

"I Was Born To Be A Queen"

"Uncrowned But Not Unshaken:
The Legacy of Queen Vashti"

But in this situation, I believe something more personal was at play.

My thought is that King Xerxes allowed others to influence a decision that should have remained between him and his wife. Why? Perhaps he felt embarrassed when Queen Vashti refused his request in front of his nobles. Maybe his pride was wounded, and instead of handling the matter privately or with grace, he turned to his advisers to help him save face. It's possible that Queen Vashti could have approached her refusal differently perhaps with more discretion or softer words but when a woman is asked to compromise her dignity, her response may come from a place of deep conviction.

Still, at the end of the day, beyond the layers of politics, pride, and power, I believe this moment was part of God's greater plan.

As I studied this passage, I asked myself: *Could it be that King Xerxes wasn't trying to shame his queen, but wanted to share her beauty with others out of admiration and pride? Or did Queen Vashti feel dishonored by the request to be paraded before a room full of intoxicated men?* These are valid perspectives, and both could be true. But speaking as a woman, I can certainly understand why Queen Vashti may have felt disrespected. Her worth was far greater than her physical

"I Was Born To Be A Queen"

beauty, and perhaps she knew that no crown was worth compromising her identity or values.

"This is when I had to put on my spiritual glasses."

Because while this story may seem like a tragic ending for Queen Vashti, I believe it was a divine setup for something far greater. God had a plan. A plan that required a shift in the palace. A plan that opened the door for Queen Esther to rise and fulfill her purpose to save her people and be a vessel for God's deliverance.

When God has a great plan, it rarely unfolds the way we expect. It often challenges our comfort, confronts our assumptions, and calls us to trust Him beyond what we can see. That's what I see in this story not just a king, a queen, and a kingdom, but a divine orchestration of events that positioned the right people, at the right time, for the right purpose.

So yes, King Xerxes had the power. Queen Vashti made a bold choice. And while the human side of the story is filled with emotion and questions, the spiritual side reveals a sovereign God working behind the scenes for our good and His glory.

"I Was Born To Be A Queen"

"A Woman Then and Now: Reflecting Through the Lens of Queen Vashti."

Throughout this book, I will take you on a journey that explores what it truly meant to be a woman during Queen Vashti's time and what it means to be a woman today. While centuries may separate us from the Persian Empire, the struggles, expectations, and complexities of womanhood remain ever relevant. By examining Queen Vashti's story, we are given a powerful lens through which to understand the strength, dignity, and voice of women across generations.

In Queen Vashti's time, women especially those in royal courts were often viewed as symbols of beauty, status, and obedience. Their value was closely tied to their appearance, their ability to produce heirs, and their willingness to submit to authority particularly the authority of men. A queen, despite her royal title, was still expected to comply with the king's wishes without question. To refuse the king was not only unthinkable but dangerous. It could cost a woman everything her crown, her position, and her very life.

And yet, Queen Vashti did the unthinkable. She said *No*.

"I Was Born To Be A Queen"

"Uncrowned But Not Unshaken: The Legacy of Queen Vashti"

That simple act has sparked centuries of debate. Some view her refusal as rebellion and disrespect. They argue that her decision undermined the authority of the king and disrupted order. Others, however, see her as a courageous trailblazer a woman who stood up for her dignity in a moment when she was being asked to compromise it.

Both perspectives deserve to be heard, because the truth is: the story of Queen Vashti is layered and complex. She was a woman navigating power, expectation, and personal conviction. And just like many women today, she was faced with a difficult decision that tested her values, her voice, and her worth.

As we walk through this book together, we'll reflect not only on Queen Vashti's time but also on how her story parallels the experiences of modern women. Today, women continue to face pressure to conform, to be silent, to shrink in the presence of power. We are still challenged to find our voice in systems that don't always honor it. Yet like Queen Vashti we are also called to rise to speak up, to stand firm, and to trust that obedience to our values is never in vain.

Some will argue that Queen Vashti was wrong. Others will say she was right. But what matters most is the impact of her decision. She chose dignity over comfort. She chose purpose over position. And in doing so, she became a symbol of quiet strength and inner conviction.

"I Was Born To Be A Queen"

"Uncrowned But Not Unshaken:
The Legacy of Queen Vashti"

As you read on, I encourage you to think deeply about what it means to be a woman not just in biblical times, but in today's world. What choices are we being asked to make? Where are we being called to stand? What does it look like to honor God with our courage and integrity?

Whether you agree with Queen Vashti's decision or not, one truth remains: her story opens the door for important conversations about identity, purpose, and the divine plans that unfold through our willingness to trust God no matter the cost.

"I Was Born To Be A Queen"

The Queen's Response to Her King

When I began writing this book about Queen Vashti, I was firmly convinced that she had been wronged disrespected and dishonored by her own husband, King Xerxes. I couldn't understand why such a woman of strength and grace would be stripped of her crown for simply saying "no." I questioned what God was doing in this story. But as I leaned in and began to see through spiritual eyes, putting on what I call my "spiritual glasses," a deeper truth began to unfold a truth not just about a woman's courage, but about God's greater plan.

Let's begin by examining King Xerxes' request. The king, in a moment of intoxication and celebration, called for Queen Vashti to appear before his guests to display her beauty. He was surrounded by nobles and officials, men whose opinions clearly held weight.

Though he was the king and had the authority to decide alone, he allowed his counselors to influence the future of his wife. This raises a few possibilities for me. Was he truly trying to honor his queen by showing off her beauty.

"I Was Born To Be A Queen"

Or was he, under the influence of alcohol and ego, subjecting her to public humiliation?

As a woman, I can deeply empathize with Queen Vashti. Her response was not simply about defiance it was about dignity. She too was hosting a banquet for the women of the palace, and I imagine those women were not silent. Knowing the way women encourage one another, I can hear their voices echoing around her: "You are the Queen! You don't have to go out there like that. Stand up for yourself and for all of us!"

So, she did.

Though it was unpopular, even dangerous, Queen Vashti chose to say "no." She stood her ground. She made the decision to put her foot down in a moment when her voice mattered most. She wasn't just standing for herself she became an example of integrity, strength, and self-respect for other women, both then and now. Yes, her decision came with consequences. But she was willing to pay the price to protect her honor.

Why did all this take place?

Because God had a bigger plan.

"I Was Born To Be A Queen"

"Uncrowned But Not Unshaken: The Legacy of Queen Vashti"

The truth is, when God is orchestrating something for His glory and for the salvation of His people, we don't always understand it. It doesn't always make sense. It can feel uncomfortable and even unfair. But Queen Vashti's removal wasn't just a result of royal drama it was divinely allowed to make room for another woman, Queen Esther, to rise and fulfill her purpose in the salvation of the Jewish people.

I believe that during her time as queen, Vashti came to know God. She may not have been part of the Jewish lineage, but I believe she had an encounter with the God of purpose. She was willing to step aside, to let go of position and title, and embrace the unknown, because she trusted that there was something greater at work. And God honored her obedience not by public praise, but by allowing her to leave with her dignity intact and her head held high.

God closed the door for one queen and opened it for another.

Throughout this book, we will explore not just the historical context of Queen Vashti's decision, but what it means to be a woman then and now. We'll dive into themes of honor, courage, obedience, and identity. And while there may be differing views some may believe that Queen Vashti was rebellious while others see her as righteous the

"I Was Born To Be A Queen"

most important take away is that God's plan prevailed. At the end of the day, it wasn't about who was right or wrong. It was about who was positioned for purpose. Vashti's exit was Esther's entrance, and both women played their roles with courage.

May this reflection help you see beyond the surface and inspire you to trust God's plan for your life even when it doesn't make sense.

"I Was Born To Be A Queen"

1 Am Doing A New Thing

Isaiah 43:19

"See, I am doing a new thing! Now it springs up; do you not perceive it? I am making a way in the wilderness and streams in the wasteland."

This scripture says a lot about how God was doing a *new thing* in the lives of two women He used to change the course of history Queen Vashti and Queen Esther. Their stories reflect the power of divine transition, courage, and purpose. Often, when God is about to do something new, it may require us to take a bold step one that challenges tradition, defies expectations, and pulls us out of our comfort zone. That's exactly what He did with these two remarkable women.

Queen Vashti's refusal to obey King Xerxes' demeaning command was not an act of rebellion, but a stand for dignity, integrity, and self-respect. She risked everything her crown, her position, and her future for the sake of what she believed was right.

"I Was Born To Be A Queen"

That single act, though it cost her everything in the natural, became the gateway for a divine shift. Her courage created space for Queen Esther to rise. It's a powerful reminder that when one door closes, it may not be the end, but the beginning of a new era in God's redemptive story.

To walk into the new thing God has for us often requires risk. It may mean losing familiar comforts, positions, or relationships. But the question remains: Which risk are you willing to take to fulfill the destiny God has placed on your life? Are you willing to lose everything in the eyes of the world in order to gain everything in the eyes of God?

Though the Bible does not give details about what became of Queen Vashti, many scholars and traditions suggest she lived out her life in exile, stripped of royal power and influence. But I choose to believe she lived with peace in her heart, knowing she had stood for righteousness. I believe she had no regrets, for she was a woman of strength and courage who played a crucial role in the unfolding of God's greater plan.

Queen Vashti may have exited the palace, but she entered the pages of divine history as a woman of principle. And just like her, when we stand for what is right even at great personal cost we align ourselves with God's bigger picture. We become part of His master plan. And in

"I Was Born To Be A Queen"

that plan, God never forgets or forsakes those who take a righteous stand.

Queen Vashti's legacy reminds us of that obedience to God's truth and faith in His sovereignty always lead to divine provision and purpose even if the world never sees it. Just remember God is doing a new thing!

Answer These Questions:

Can you recognize the new thing God is doing in your life right now?

Are you willing to take a bold risk, like Queen Vashti, even if it means losing everything to stand for what's right?

Do you trust that God can restore and even multiply everything you've lost?

"I Was Born To Be A Queen"

"Uncrowned But Not Unshaken:
The Legacy of Queen Vashti"

Do you believe that Queen Vashti was divinely positioned to play a crucial role in the unfolding of God's greater plan?

Prayer:

Lord, thank You for being the Author of new beginnings. Thank You for showing me through the lives of women like Queen Vashti and Queen Esther that sometimes I must take a bold step of faith even when it's uncomfortable, unfamiliar, or unpopular to walk into the new thing You are doing in my life. Remind me, Lord, that true change often requires courage and that with You, I am never walking alone.

In Jesus' Name, Amen.

"I Was Born To Be A Queen"

I Will Not Compromise Just To Fit In

A powerful scripture that speaks to the theme **"I will not compromise to just fit in"** is:

Romans 12:2 (NIV):
"Do not conform to the pattern of this world but be transformed by the renewing of your mind. Then you will be able to test and approve what God's will is—his good, pleasing and perfect will."

Reflection:

This verse encourages us not to bend, bow, or change ourselves just to blend in with the world's standards or expectations. Instead, we are called to be transformed set apart by aligning our minds and hearts with God's truth. Refusing to compromise may cost us temporary comfort or acceptance, but it brings eternal alignment with God's will.

"I Will Not Compromise Myself Just To Fit In."

"I Was Born To Be A Queen"

"Uncrowned But Not Unshaken:
The Legacy of Queen Vashti"

This scripture aligns perfectly with the story of Queen Vashti, a woman of bold conviction who refused to conform to the expectations of a worldly system that demanded her obedience at the cost of her dignity. When King Xerxes commanded Queen Vashti to present herself before a room of intoxicated men simply to display her beauty, she refused. Her decision to say "no" was not just about personal pride it was a refusal to compromise her values and identity just to retain a title.

Queen Vashti chose integrity over influence, dignity over acceptance, and truth over tradition. She was not willing to sacrifice her self-worth to remain in a position that demanded she become less than who God created her to be. In doing so, she stood as a timeless example of what it means to reject conformity to the world's standards.

We live in a time where fitting in often means watering down our beliefs, compromising our values, or going along with what's popular even when it goes against God's Word. But as believers, we are called to be different. We are called to be set apart. When we compromise ourselves to fit in, we may gain temporary approval from people, but we risk falling out of alignment with God's will.

Queen Vashti's story teaches us that sometimes standing for what is right means walking away from what is familiar. It may cost us titles, relationships, or comfort but

"I Was Born To Be A Queen"

it never costs us God's presence. He honors those who honor Him.

So let this be your declaration:

"I will not compromise myself just fit in. I will stand for what is right, even if I must stand alone. I will follow God's will, not the world's ways. I will be transformed, not conformed."

Like Queen Vashti, may we all have the courage to choose righteousness over recognition and obedience over acceptance, knowing that when we stand for God, He stands with us.

Answer These Questions:

Are you willing to stay true to yourself, even if it means not pleasing others?

Have there been times when you compromised your values to gain acceptance or avoid conflict?

"I Was Born To Be A Queen"

"Uncrowned But Not Unshaken: The Legacy of Queen Vashti"

Do you have the confidence to stand up for what is right, even when it's unpopular?

What lessons or personal revelations did you gain from Queen Vashti's story?

Prayer:

Lord, help me to stay focused and rooted in Your truth. Strengthen me so that I will not compromise my values just to fit in or be accepted by the world. Remind me daily of the importance of seeking You in all things and trusting that You are my provider, my source, and my guide. When things aren't going the way I expected, increase my faith and help me to keep my eyes on You. Lead me with Your wisdom, and help me walk in boldness, obedience, and unwavering trust.

In Jesus' Name, Amen.

"I Was Born To Be A Queen"

I Will Be The Voice For All Women

Proverbs 31:8-9 (NIV):

"Speak up for those who cannot speak for themselves, for the rights of all who are destitute. Speak up and judge fairly; defend the rights of the poor and needy."

Reflection:

This scripture is a divine call to advocacy, compassion, and justice. It encourages us to be a voice for the voiceless, to speak out on behalf of those who are overlooked, oppressed, or silenced. When you declare, *"I will be the voice for all women,"* you are stepping into a biblical mandate to defend, uplift, and empower others especially those who have been pushed to the margins.

I Will Be the Voice for All Women"

I believe that when Queen Vashti made the bold decision to stand up for her rights, she became a voice for all women past, present, and future. Her refusal to be objectified and disrespected was more than an act of personal

"I Was Born To Be A Queen"

dignity; it was a declaration of self-worth that echoed far beyond the walls of the Persian palace. In a time when women were expected to remain silent and submissive, Queen Vashti's courage shattered expectations and made room for a new narrative one of strength, identity, and purpose.

When we understand the importance of speaking up, we will begin to walk in the same power that Queen Vashti displayed. We become the voice for women who are not yet strong enough to speak for themselves, and for those who are still silenced by fear, oppression, or shame. Speaking up isn't always easy; many of us remember seasons when we didn't have the confidence, the language, or the support to use our voice. But it was through the boldness of another through someone else's testimony, someone else's stand that we learned we too could rise.

This is the heart of Queen Vashti's journey. Her story is not just about a queen who lost her crown it's about a woman who chose her character over her comfort. She may have been removed from the throne, but she took her place in the lineage of world changers. Her voice still speaks.

Let her journey inspire you to embrace your own. Decide today to be the voice for all women. Speak up for jus-

"I Was Born To Be A Queen"

tice, for dignity, for righteousness. Share your story so that others can find theirs. Advocate for the overlooked, the unheard, the wounded. Just as Queen Vashti paved the way for Queen Esther, your voice may be the catalyst for someone else's rise.

You are not just speaking for yourself. You are speaking for the next generations.

Answer These Questions:

Do you believe you have the power to be a voice for other women?

Do you see Queen Vashti as a bold voice on behalf of all women?

Are you willing to stand up and speak for young women who feel voiceless or unheard?

"I Was Born To Be A Queen"

"Uncrowned But Not Unshaken: The Legacy of Queen Vashti"

Do you have the confidence to advocate for yourself and your values?

Prayer:

Lord, thank You for reminding me that I do have a voice one that is powerful, purposeful, and needed in this world. Thank You for awakening the strength within me to speak not only on my behalf but also on behalf of women who feel voiceless, overlooked, or silenced. I am grateful for the confidence You have planted in my heart a confidence that is not rooted in the opinions of others but in the truth of who You say I am. Thank You for equipping me to defend my rights with grace, courage, and conviction. Continue to lead me as I walk boldly in the calling You've placed on my life and help me to be a light for others who are searching for theirs.

In Jesus' Name, Amen.

"I Was Born To Be A Queen"

I Will Stand Up For Justice

Isaiah 1:17 (NIV):

"Learn to do right; seek justice. Defend the oppressed. Take up the cause of the fatherless; plead the case of the widow."

Reflection:

This verse is a direct call from God to pursue justice, righteousness, and compassion. To stand up for justice means to actively confront wrongdoing, defend the vulnerable, and be a voice for the voiceless. It's not just a moral choice it's a spiritual mandate. When you declare, *"I will stand up for justice,"* you align yourself with God's heart for truth, fairness, and mercy. You become a vessel of His justice in a broken world.

"In This World Where There Is So Much Injustice."

In a world overwhelmed with injustice, oppression, and inequality, it can often feel daunting to take a stand. Fear, uncertainty, or isolation can silence even the strongest voices. But in moments like these, we are reminded of

"I Was Born To Be A Queen"

53

women like Queen Vashti, who chose to stand up not just for herself, but for what was right in the eyes of God.

Let us remember that Queen Vashti lived in a time and culture where women had little to no voice, yet she refused to compromise her dignity. When summoned by King Xerxes to display her beauty before a room of intoxicated men, she stood her ground and said "no." That decision cost her everything she had in the natural realm her crown, her title, her royal position but it marked her as a woman of honor, courage, and deep spiritual conviction. She recognized that the injustice in her own life could no longer be ignored. Her act of defiance was not rebellion it was *alignment*. Alignment with the truth. Alignment with integrity. Alignment with God's heart for justice.

We must take the same posture:

When we choose to stand up for justice whether in our homes, churches, communities, or globally we are aligning ourselves with the heart of God, who is the very definition of justice. As Isaiah 1:17 says, *"Learn to do right; seek justice. Defend the oppressed.*

Take up the cause of the fatherless; plead the case of the widow." This is not a suggestion; it is a divine assignment.

"I Was Born To Be A Queen"

"Uncrowned But Not Unshaken: The Legacy of Queen Vashti"

The dictionary defines standing up for justice as *advocating for fairness, equality, and the protection of rights within a community or society.* It is the embodiment of moral courage and the active pursuit of what is right and equitable for all individuals. Queen Vashti embodied this truth. Though she may not have had the language of modern day advocacy, her actions spoke volumes.

I want you to trust God the way she did. I want you to remember that your voice matters. When you speak out against injustice when you stand for righteousness you are doing more than expressing an opinion. You are fulfilling a spiritual calling.

So, take courage. Use your voice. Be the light. Be the advocate. Be the reflection of God's justice in a broken world. Just like Queen Vashti, your stand might come with a cost but it also comes with divine purpose.

Answer These Questions:

How important is it to you to stand up for justice, even when it comes at a personal cost?

"I Was Born To Be A Queen"

"Uncrowned But Not Unshaken: The Legacy of Queen Vashti"

Have you taken time to read and reflect on the story of Queen Esther and Queen Vashti?

What are your thoughts on the challenges women faced during Queen Vashti's time?

In a world often dominated by men, do you believe there is still hope and progress for us as women today?

Prayer:

Lord, help us to walk in the confidence that You have placed within us as women of purpose and strength. Give us the boldness to stand up for what is right, even when it's difficult or unpopular. Teach us to trust You fully in every situation, knowing that appearances may be deceived, but You are always working on our behalf. Remind us that You are the God who fights for Your people and defends those who stand in truth. Strengthen our hearts, sharpen our vision, and guide our steps as we walk in alignment with Your will.

In Jesus' Name, Amen.

"I Was Born To Be A Queen"

I Will Honor My Body

1 Corinthians 6:19-20 (NIV):
"Do you not know that your bodies are temples of the Holy Spirit, who is in you, whom you have received from God? You are not your own; you were bought at a price. Therefore, honor God with your bodies."

Reflection:

This verse reminds us that our bodies are not ordinary they are sacred vessels that carry the Spirit of God. Honoring your body means caring for it, respecting it, and using it in ways that glorify Him. Whether it's through healthy living, purity, rest, or self-respect, choosing to honor your body is choosing to honor the One who created it.

Queen Vashti: A Woman Who Honored Her Body and Her Worth

Queen Vashti stands as a timeless example of what it means to honor one's body and walk in dignity.

"I Was Born To Be A Queen"

"Uncrowned But Not Unshaken: The Legacy of Queen Vashti"

When she refused King Xerxes' command to display her beauty before a gathering of drunken men, she was making a bold statement: *My body is not a trophy. My worth is not defined by the gaze of others.* Though she was queen, she chose character over crown, modesty over popularity, and purpose over pressure.

Queen Vashti understood that her body was a temple a sacred vessel given by God. She chose to guard it with honor and refused to let it be paraded or reduced to an object or spectacle. That decision was not just about personal dignity; it was an act of reverence for the God who created her. She knew that true royalty is not about how much skin is shown, but how much strength and self-worth is carried within.

In today's world, where social pressure and cultural trends often push women to reveal more to feel seen or valued, we must look to women like Queen Vashti women who understand that modesty is not weakness, but protection. It is a shield of wisdom that says, *I know my worth, and I don't need to reveal everything to prove it.*

I recently read something that powerfully captured my attention.

"Sometimes, the attention you're getting isn't because you're 'too fine' or 'too hot.' It's because you've left yourself uncovered.

"I Was Born To Be A Queen"

"Uncrowned But Not Unshaken:
The Legacy of Queen Vashti"

Modesty doesn't hide your beauty it protects it. You don't need to reveal everything to feel valued. Let your presence speak louder than your skin."

— Unknown

Dear Queens,

You were created with divine beauty, purpose, and grace. Your value doesn't increase by the number of likes or stares you receive. It shines brightest when you carry yourself with dignity and walk in the knowledge that you are fearfully and wonderfully made (Psalm 139:14).

Let your fashion reflect your faith. Let your elegance speak louder than any trend.

As the Bible reminds us in John 17:16, *"They are not of the world, even as I am not of it."* We may live in this world, but we are called to live differently to be the light of this world, and to be examples, to be Queens who honor their bodies, just like Queen Vashti. So, wear your crown with modesty, grace, and confidence knowing that true beauty comes not from what is exposed, but from what is esteemed.

"I Was Born To Be A Queen"

Answer These Questions:

In what ways do you honor and respect your body as God's temple?

What do you believe that your body, mind, and spirit needs to thrive?

Are you caring for your temple in a way that reflects health and wholeness?

Does your personal style and fashion reflect your faith and values?

"I Was Born To Be A Queen"

"Uncrowned But Not Unshaken:
The Legacy of Queen Vashti"

Prayer:

Lord, show me how to honor my body as the sacred temple You created it to be. Teach me to treat it with the care, respect, and love that reflects Your heart.

Help me not to seek validation through likes, attention, or approval from others, but to find my worth in You alone. Let my true beauty shine through the way I carry myself with dignity, wisdom, and confidence knowing that I am fearfully and wonderfully made, just as Your Word declares in Psalm 139:14.

In Jesus' Name, Amen.

"I Was Born To Be A Queen"

1 Am Willing To Pay The Price For A Greater Calling

This is a powerful scripture emphasizing the willingness to pay a higher price for your faith.

Luke 9:23, which states, "If any of you wants to be my follower, you must give up your own way, take up your cross daily, and follow me."

Queen Vashti Was Willing to Pay the Price for a Greater Calling:

Queen Vashti's story is one of courage, conviction, and calling. In a moment of pressure, when the world around her demanded compliance, she chose dignity over disgrace, purpose over popularity, and honor over humiliation. Vashti refused to be paraded before a room of drunken men to satisfy the pride and arrogance of a king and his court. She understood the value of her identity, her body, and her role not just as queen, but as a woman fearfully and wonderfully made by God.

"I Was Born To Be A Queen"

"Uncrowned But Not Unshaken: The Legacy of Queen Vashti"

Queen Vashti's decision came at a cost. She lost her crown, her position, and her place in the palace. But what she gained was far greater: the assurance that she had stood for something meaningful, the silent strength of being true to herself and a role in God's unfolding divine plan. Her refusal paved the way for Queen Esther, who was a woman of faith and courage, that would rise to her calling.

There are so many times in life when we, too, must be willing to *pay the price* for a greater calling in Christ Jesus. That calling might require us to speak truth when it's easier to remain silent, to stand firm when others bow to culture, and to obey God when disobedience is more convenient. Queen Vashti reminds us that not every sacrifice is because of wrongdoing some consequences come because of righteousness. And those are the most meaningful.

The reality is obedience comes with a cost. Sometimes we lose relationships, opportunities, status, or comfort. But Jesus said in Matthew 16:24, *"If anyone desires to come after Me, let him deny himself, and take up his cross, and follow Me."* That's not a call to comfort it's a call to courage.

Queen Vashti's story challenges us today: How many of us are willing to make the unpopular decision to honor God and ourselves, even when others won't understand it? Are we willing to lose the approval of man to keep the

"I Was Born To Be A Queen"

approval of God? Will we risk being rejected so that we can walk in purpose?

Queen Vashti's stand was not rebellion it was reverence. It was her willingness to say, *"I know who I am. I will not allow anyone to misuse the temple God has given me."* She understood that sometimes the price of obedience is steep, but the reward of integrity and divine alignment is priceless.

Let us follow her example and be faithful not popular, not pleasing to the crowd, but faithful to the ways of God. Let us be women and men of unshakable conviction, willing to pay the price for a greater calling. For in the end, it is not the earthly crown that matters most it is the eternal reward of walking in God's will.

Answer These Questions:

Are you willing to make sacrifices in order to pursue the greater calling God has placed on your life?

Do you believe Queen Vashti was willing to pay the price to walk in integrity and purpose?

"I Was Born To Be A Queen"

"Uncrowned But Not Unshaken:
The Legacy of Queen Vashti"

Are you willing to make the unpopular choice if it means honoring God and staying true to yourself?

Are you prepared to lose the approval of people in order to remain faithful to the approval of God?

Prayer:

Lord, help me to see how important it is to seek Your approval above all else, not the fleeting validation of others. Give me the strength and courage to pay the price for standing up for what is right, even when it's difficult and not popular. Teach me to walk in Your righteousness and follow Your will, knowing that true fulfillment comes from obedience.

In Jesus' Name, Amen.

"I Was Born To Be A Queen"

1 Will Honor God In All That 1 Do

Colossians 3:17
"And whatever you do, in word or deed, do everything in the name of the Lord Jesus, giving thanks to God the Father through him. "This verse emphasizes that all actions should be done with a heart of gratitude and in the name of Jesus.

1 Peter 4:11
"If anyone speaks, he should do it as one who speaks the very words of God. If anyone serves, he should do it with the strength God provides, so that in all things God may be praised through Jesus Christ. To him be the glory and the power for ever and ever. Amen." This verse focuses on using our words and actions to glorify God.

Psalms 86:12
"I will praise you, Lord my God, with all my heart; I will glorify your name forever. "This verse expresses a heart of worship and dedication to God's glory.

The Word of God clearly reveals the importance of honoring Him in all that we do. From our thoughts to our

"I Was Born To Be A Queen"

actions, we are called to reflect His love, kindness, and grace. When we operate with gratitude, speak words of affirmation, and live with humility, we glorify God and show our reverence for who He is. Scriptures like Colossians 3:17 remind us, *"And whatever you do, whether in word or deed, do it all in the name of the Lord Jesus, giving thanks to God the Father through him."* Every act of love, every kind word, and every grateful heart is a form of worship that brings glory to God.

Honoring God Through Courageous Conviction: The Example of Queen Vashti

There comes a point in every believer's life where we must truly understand that everything, we do should be done to glorify God. Our actions, decisions, and how we carry ourselves should reflect our reverence for Him. Honoring our bodies is one such sacred act of glorifying God recognizing that our bodies are temples of the Holy Spirit (1 Corinthians 6:19-20). When we refuse to allow others to disrespect us, we are not just standing up for ourselves we are honoring God in a profound and powerful way.

Queen Vashti exemplified this truth. When she refused King Xerxes' request to parade herself before his drunken guests, she wasn't simply rejecting a command she was making a bold statement of integrity and self-worth. Her decision was an act of worship, an offering to God that declared, "I will not dishonor the vessel You created." It was a courageous stand that echoed throughout the kingdom, a declaration that her dignity and honor were not for sale, not even to please a king.

Queen Vashti's actions remind us that we cannot live our lives based on the opinions of others. She was not concerned with what the king's friends thought, nor was she moved by the fear of consequences. Her focus was on doing what was right in God's eyes and what was right for herself as a woman, a queen, and a leader. She understood that as queen, she had a responsibility not only to herself but to the women in the palace who looked up to her. Her choice was not made in isolation it was made with the awareness that her influence mattered.

Queen Vashti's refusal was not rebellion; it was a righteous stand. It was an act of leadership, a moment where she chose reverence over reputation. In choosing to protect her body, she set a standard for every woman who ever questioned their worth. She proved that honor, dignity, and godliness must not be compromised for acceptance or popularity.

Let her example be a reminder that honoring God may cost you something, but it will never cost you your purpose.

"I Was Born To Be A Queen"

"Uncrowned But Not Unshaken: The Legacy of Queen Vashti"

Sometimes, standing for righteousness requires standing alone but it always positions you for divine favor. Queen Vashti stood for something greater than herself and in doing so, she glorified God.

Answer These Questions:

In what ways do you honor God through your actions, choices, and daily life?

Do you ever feel conflicted or labeled as rebellious when you stand up for what is right?

Are you able to stay true to your values without being influenced by the opinions of others?

Do you find yourself concerned about how others perceive your decisions and beliefs?

"I Was Born To Be A Queen"

Prayer:

Lord, help me to remember that I must honor You in all that I do. Strengthen me to never shy away from doing what is right, even when it's not easy. Let my actions, words, and choices reflect Your love and truth. When I honor You in every area of my life, may it draw others closer to You and bring glory to Your Holy Name.

In Jesus' Name, Amen.

"I Was Born To Be A Queen"

Myself Worth Means Everything

Psalm 139:14 (NIV):
"I praise you because I am fearfully and wonderfully made; your works are wonderful; I know that full well."

This verse reminds us that our worth comes from being intentionally and beautifully created by God. Knowing who you are in Him gives you the confidence to walk in purpose, value, and dignity because your self-worth means everything to the One who made you.

"Queen Vashti: A Portrait of Self-Worth and Courage."

Queen Vashti's story is one of boldness, dignity, and unwavering self-respect. Her self-worth meant everything to her so much so that she was willing to give up her title, her position, and her comfort for the sake of what she believed was right. In the face of royal pressure and public scrutiny, Queen Vashti chose to stand for her personal value rather than be reduced to a spectacle for the king's guests. Her decision was not one of rebellion,

"I Was Born To Be A Queen"

but of reverence for herself, her body, and the God who created her.

In today's world, we need more women like Queen Vashti women who know their worth is not for sale. Women who understand that their value does not come from titles, popularity, or approval from others, but from the divine hand that shaped them. Queen Vashti's stand reminds us that our purpose, value, and dignity are worth everything. She modeled what it means to protect your God-given identity, even when it comes at a high cost.

God's Word confirms this truth in **Psalm 139:14**, which says: *"I praise you because I am fearfully and wonderfully made; your works are wonderful, I know that full well."* Queen Vashti lived out this truth. She didn't need applause or acceptance to validate her worth she knew it full well. Her strength came from an inner conviction, a quiet confidence that refused to be silenced or shamed.

There are so many things in this world that attempt to pull at our self-worth cultural pressures, comparison, rejection, and fear. But the key to holding on to our identity is staying focused on *who God has called us to be.* Queen Vashti understood this. She understood that her actions had meaning, that her voice mattered, and that the example she set could impact not just the women in the palace, but generations to come.

"I Was Born To Be A Queen"

"Uncrowned But Not Unshaken: The Legacy of Queen Vashti"

I believe she had no fear when she responded to the king's request. Her courage came from knowing who she was. She didn't crumble under pressure; she stood tall in purpose. And in doing so, she left behind a legacy of bravery and value.

Queen Vashti's story is not just history it's a divine reminder to every woman: Never fear standing up for what is right. Your self-worth is a gift from God. Protect it. Walk in it. Honor it. Because when you know who you are in Him, you'll never settle for anything less.

Answer These Questions:

What does your self-worth mean to you on a personal and spiritual level?

What actions do you take to affirm and stand up for your self-worth?

"I Was Born To Be A Queen"

"Uncrowned But Not Unshaken: The Legacy of Queen Vashti"

How do you guard and protect your self-worth in difficult situations?

Are you able to stand confidently for your self-worth without fear or hesitation?

Prayer:

Lord, help me to see the importance of my self-worth and to remember that it is not up for sale. Remind me daily that I am fearfully and wonderfully made by You. Help me keep my eyes totally focused on You and not be swayed by the opinions or pressures of others. Let Queen Vashti be a beautiful example of courage, dignity, and strength allow her story to show us how to stand firm in who You've called us to be.

In Jesus' Name, Amen.

"I Was Born To Be A Queen"

I Shall Rise Above The Pain

Isaiah 61:3 (NIV)

"...to bestow on them a crown of beauty instead of ashes, the oil of joy instead of mourning, and a garment of praise instead of a spirit of despair. They will be called oaks of righteousness, a planting of the Lord for the display of his splendor."

This verse is a reminder that God can take our deepest pain and transform it into purpose, beauty, and strength. Even in seasons of mourning and despair, He equips us to rise above with dignity and divine joy.

Rising Above the Pain: Lessons from Queen Vashti's Courage.

One of the things I love most about God is His divine ability to take our deepest pain and transform it into a powerful part of His greater plan. Pain never has the final say in our story when God is involved. He takes what was meant to break us and uses it to build something far more beautiful than we could ever imagine. We see this clearly in the life of Queen Vashti.

"I Was Born To Be A Queen"

"Uncrowned But Not Unshaken: The Legacy of Queen Vashti"

Queen Vashti's story is often over shadowed by Queen Esther's, yet her silent strength was just as crucial in the unfolding of God's plan. When King Xerxes commanded Queen Vashti to appear before his drunken guests to display her beauty, he wasn't asking out of love or honor he was demanding her dignity for public entertainment. Imagine the anguish she must have felt: the man she loved, her husband, asking her to do something so dishonorable and humiliating. It wasn't just a rejection of his command it was a rejection of her self-worth.

Queen Vashti chose to rise above her pain. She chose dignity over fear. She chose self-respect over approval. That one act of bravery created a space for Queen Esther to emerge and fulfill God's plan to save the Jewish people. It is a powerful reminder that God can use our most painful position for His purpose. He is a God who doesn't waste pain He repurposes it.

There are many moments in our own lives when pain shows up unexpectedly through betrayal, rejection, loss, or disappointment. Like Queen Vashti, we must make the choice to rise.

But how?

"I Was Born To Be A Queen"

Here are a few ways to rise above your pain:

1. **Talk to God About It**
   Begin with God. Pour out your heart to Him. He is close to the brokenhearted and listens when we cry out. Don't pretend you're not hurting acknowledge your pain in prayer and allow Him to meet you there.

2. **Lean on Someone You Trust**
   God created us for community. Find a trusted friend, mentor, pastor, or counselor to talk to. Sometimes healing comes through conversations that help us process what we're feeling.

3. **Take Time to Be Still**
   Stillness is powerful. Give yourself permission to pause, to reflect, and to feel. In that quiet space, God can bring clarity, comfort, and renewed strength. This is likely what Queen Vashti did— she took the time to reflect before standing firm in her decision.

4. **Stand Firm in Your Worth**
   Your value is not defined by what others ask of you but by the One who created you. Queen Vashti remembered who she was, and her refusal

"I Was Born To Be A Queen"

became a testament to that truth. You are fearfully and wonderfully made walk in that identity.

5. **Trust God's Bigger Plan**
   You may not see it now, but God is working behind the scenes. Queen Vashti couldn't have known that her decision would open the door for Esther to become queen and ultimately save a nation. Your stand may be setting up something extraordinary too.

In the end, Queen Vashti's pain carried a purpose and so does yours. God is the Master of transformation, turning heartbreak into healing, rejection into redirection, and pain into purpose. Even the most shattered pieces of our lives can be placed in His hands and used to build something glorious. So today, make the choice to rise not because the journey is easy, but because you know Who walks beside you.

Answer These Questions:

How significant is it for you to confront your pain and rise above it?

"Uncrowned But Not Unshaken: The Legacy of Queen Vashti"

Do you feel comfortable discussing your pain with God?

Do you trust that God has a greater plan for your life?

Do you recognize that sometimes the most healing step is to simply be still?

Prayer:

Lord, thank You for showing me how to rise above my pain. Thank You for reminding me that You will love me through every moment of heartache and uncertainty. Just as You loved Queen Vashti through her pain, You are loving me through mine. Thank You for the strength to stand, the grace to heal, and the vision to see the bigger plans You have for my life. I trust You, Lord, and I surrender my pain into Your hands. Amen.

"I Was Born To Be A Queen"

I Am Willing To Step Aside

A powerful scripture that reflects the heart of being willing to **step aside**, whether for God's greater plan, someone else's calling, or in humility and obedience, is found in **John 3:30 (NIV):**

"He must become greater; I must become less."
(John 3:30)

This verse was spoken by John the Baptist when he recognized it was time for Jesus to take center stage. It is a beautiful expression of humility, purpose, and surrender being willing to step aside so that God's will and glory can be revealed through someone else.

If you're looking for additional reinforcement, consider:

"Do nothing out of selfish ambition or vain conceit. Rather, in humility value others above yourselves."
(Philippians 2:3, NIV)

"I Was Born To Be A Queen"

My dear friend sent me this quote which truly speaks Volume of who this amazing woman was.

Don't sleep On Queen Vashti, She wasn't just the woman before Queen Esther. She was the woman who refused to be degraded so another could be elevated. Her 'No" was the seed that made room for deliverance.

Queen Vashti: A Woman Who Stepped Aside with Power and Purpose

Queen Vashti was not simply a woman who defied a king she was a woman who defined dignity. In a time when women were expected to be silent, compliant, and objectified, Queen Vashti stood as a pillar of strength, refusing to be degraded for the entertainment of others. Her decision to step aside was not an act of rebellion it was an act of resistance, an assertion of self-worth, and a bold declaration that she was more than a beautiful face to be paraded before drunken men.

She chose her values over validation. Her dignity over a title. Her integrity over comfort. And in doing so, she paved the way for countless women who came after her. When others were silent, Queen Vashti spoke up. When others remained seated, Queen Vashti stood. And when others accepted what was expected, Queen Vashti challenged it.

"I Was Born To Be A Queen"

"Uncrowned But Not Unshaken:
The Legacy of Queen Vashti"

She made the ultimate sacrifice not only for herself, but for generations of women who needed an example of what it looks like to stand firm in self-respect, even at great cost.

Throughout history, she has been labeled disobedient, rebellious, and dishonorable. But what if she was simply righteous? What if she were the first woman in recorded history to declare enough is enough. I believe the question she asked herself was, "If I don't stand up for myself, who will?" Her courage was not rooted in pride but in principle. She chose to step aside rather than compromise her soul.

In the male-dominated world we still live in today, Queen Vashti's story remains relevant. Women are often under-valued, underpaid, and overlooked. We are passed over for opportunities despite our qualifications, questioned in our competence despite our experience, and too often silenced when we speak truth to power. But just like Queen Vashti, we are not powerless.

We fix this by *using our voices*. We rise by *creating our own spaces*, building our own companies, platforms, and legacies. We come together, empower one another, and lift each other up. We push against the walls that try to confine us and build bridges for those who will come behind us.

"I Was Born To Be A Queen"

"Uncrowned But Not Unshaken: The Legacy of Queen Vashti"

Queen Vashti's act wasn't just for her it was for every woman who ever doubted her worth, questioned her value, or was told to shrink. Her legacy is not one of disobedience, but of *divine defiance* a refusal to let the world dictate her worth.

So today, may we honor Queen Vashti by living with the same fierce commitment to our dignity. May we refuse to be silenced. May we refuse to accept less. And may we always remember that stepping aside with integrity is never weakness it is *power*.

Answer These Questions:

Are you willing to step aside or make a sacrifice for a greater purpose?

How important is it to you to be a voice and advocate for other women?

Do you sometimes feel that standing up for others isn't your responsibility? (Be honest.)

"I Was Born To Be A Queen"

"Uncrowned But Not Unshaken: The Legacy of Queen Vashti"

Could you surrender everything in order to protect your dignity and self-respect?

Prayer:

Lord, help me to never forget the responsibility You have given me to always stand up for what is right. Strengthen me to be bold in truth and unwavering in righteousness, even when it is uncomfortable or unpopular. Remind me daily that I am my sister's keeper that her pain, her struggles, her victories, and her freedom matter to me. Let compassion and courage live within me so I can uplift others with grace and dignity.

Lord, keep my eyes fixed on You, for it is only through Your guidance that I can walk in integrity. When the world pulls me in different directions, anchor my heart in Your Word. May Your Spirit convict me when I am tempted to be silent or passive in the face of injustice. Empower me to be a vessel of Your love, light, and truth. Let everything, I do reflect Your heart and bring glory to Your name.

In Jesus' Name, Amen.

"I Was Born To Be A Queen"

I Will Pay Attention To The Voice Of God

Isaiah 30:21 (NIV)
"Whether you turn to the right or to the left, your ears will hear a voice behind you, saying, 'This is the way; walk in it.'"

This verse reminds us that when we choose to listen and pay attention to the voice of God, He will guide us clearly and faithfully. His voice leads us on the right path, even in times of uncertainty.

Did Queen Vashti Hear the Voice of God?

The question here could very well be: *Did Queen Vashti hear the voice of God?* I would like to boldly say *yes, she did.* Why do I say that? Because the God we serve would never lead us into situations that belittle, disgrace, or strip us of our dignity. He is a God of honor, purpose, and order. The very act of Queen Vashti standing up for herself-refusing to be paraded and objectified was, in my eyes, an act of divine clarity. It was the voice of God guiding her through a situation that required both strength and obedience to her inner conviction.

"I Was Born To Be A Queen"

"Uncrowned But Not Unshaken: The Legacy of Queen Vashti"

When Queen Vashti made her decision, she wasn't merely defying a king she was listening to something greater than royal commands. She was responding to a moral and spiritual compass that said, *"Enough is Enough."* She chose dignity over position, purpose over pressure. She might not have had a burning bush experience, but the voice of God often comes through the stillness of conviction, through the whisper that tells you: *"You are worth more than this."*

The king's advisors were quick to see the power in her refusal. They weren't just worried about Queen Vashti they were terrified that her courage would spark a revolution of self-worth among other women. And perhaps, it did. Perhaps Queen Vashti's decision gave voice to the voiceless, courage to the fearful, and strength to the silent. Her boldness had a ripple effect not just in her time, but through generations.

Even now, in this day and time, her story speaks volumes. Women everywhere are still fighting to be heard, to be valued, and to be respected. And Queen Vashti stands as a reminder that we are not to be controlled by culture, by people, or by systems that seek to silence us but only by God and by the strength He gives us within ourselves.

So, let us pay close attention to the voice of God. It may not always come with thunder or flashing lights but it

"I Was Born To Be A Queen"

will always lead us into truth, freedom, and purpose. Like Queen Vashti, may we have the courage to listen, to stand, and to inspire others to do the same.

Answer These Questions:

Do you believe Queen Vashti was guided by the voice of God in her decision?

Have you ever experienced hearing God's voice in your own life?

How do you discern and recognize when God is speaking to you?

Are you intentionally listening and paying attention to His voice in your daily walk?

"I Was Born To Be A Queen"

"Uncrowned But Not Unshaken:
The Legacy of Queen Vashti"

Prayer:

Heavenly Father, help me to always pay attention to Your Voice above the noise, above the distractions, above my own thoughts. Teach me to be still in Your presence, to quiet my mind, and to settle my spirit so that I may clearly hear the gentle whisper of Your guidance. Let my heart remain sensitive and open to Your leading, even when it's uncomfortable or inconvenient. Thank You for caring so deeply for me that You speak into my life, especially in my time of need. Your voice brings peace, direction, and reassurance. I trust You, Lord, and I choose to listen.

In Jesus' name, Amen.

"I Was Born To Be A Queen"

I Will Rise Above My Circumstances

Scripture on Rising Above Circumstances:

Isaiah 40:31 (NIV)
"But those who hope in the Lord will renew their strength. They will soar on wings like eagles; they will run and not grow weary; they will walk and not be faint."

This verse reminds us that when we place our trust and hope in God, He gives us the strength to rise above any circumstance, just as an eagle soars high above the storms.

"Queen Vashti Decided to Rise Above Her Circumstances to Stand Up for Justice"

Queen Vashti's story is a profound example of courage in the face of pressure, injustice, and potential consequence. She stood in the crossroads of a male-dominated culture, expected to obey the king's every command without question. Yet when faced with a humiliating request, she chose to rise above her circumstances and stand for

"I Was Born To Be A Queen"

what was right, even when it meant stepping into the unknown.

Her circumstance was real. She was queen, but even with her title her voice was expected to be silent. Her beauty was to be displayed like a trophy, not honored as a reflection of her dignity. When the king summoned her to parade herself before his drunken guests, Queen Vashti made a powerful decision: she said no. She stood firm, not out of rebellion, but out of a deep sense of self-worth, integrity, and justice. She chose to walk in righteousness rather than shrink in fear.

It is hard sometimes to see beyond our own circumstances. Trials, expectations, and the fear of consequence can cloud our judgement. But Queen Vashti reminds us that circumstances do not define our destiny only God does He alone gives us the power and strength to make decisions that change our situation.

Her story encourages us to trust in the guidance of God rather than temporary comfort or public approval.

In that moment of decision, Queen Vashti exemplified faith. She did not allow fear to cause her to become silent. Instead, she sought a higher truth. Psalm 32:8 says, *I will instruct you and teach you the way to go I will watch over you*

"I Was Born To Be A Queen"

"Uncrowned But Not Unshaken: The Legacy of Queen Vashti"

and I will guide you with My eyes "Queen Vashti's decision mirrors this promise. She acted with boldness, trusting that God was guiding her steps and watching over her.

Today, we can draw strength from her story. We, too, can rise above unfair treatment, cultural pressures, or moments of fear. We can seek God's wisdom in the midst of our struggles and trust that His instruction will lead us to victory. Queen Vashti may have lost her crown, but she gained something far greater her voice, her dignity, and her place in history as a woman who stood for justice when it mattered most. Her legacy challenges us all when injustice knocks on our door, justice will allow us to rise above our circumstances and trust God to lead us?

Answer These Questions:

Are you allowing your current circumstances to dictate your future?

Are you prepared to rise above the challenges you're facing?

"I Was Born To Be A Queen"

"Uncrowned But Not Unshaken: The Legacy of Queen Vashti"

Do you believe that your circumstances do not define your destiny?

Do you have the inner strength and faith to overcome what you're going through?

Prayer:

Lord, help me to see that my circumstances do not determine my destiny. Remind me daily that You, and You alone, hold the blueprint of my life in Your hands. When life feels overwhelming and I am faced with difficult choices, let me not be consumed by fear or doubt. Instead, let me lean into Your presence and trust Your divine plan.

In Jesus' Name, Amen.

"I Was Born To Be A Queen"

1 Am My Sisters Keeper

Galatians 6:2 (NIV)
"Carry each other's burdens, and in this way, you will fulfill the law of Christ."

Romans 12:10 (NLT)
"Love each other with genuine affection and take delight in honoring each other."

These verses remind us of our Christian duty to support, uplift, and walk alongside one another especially our sisters in Christ. Being your sister's keeper means to walk in love, truth, and compassion, helping her carry the weight when life gets heavy.

"I am my sister's keeper, called by God to uplift, protect, and walk beside her in love because where two or three are gathered in His name, He is there with us." *(Inspired by Matthew 18:20)*

Queen Vashti Understood What It Meant to Be Her Sister's Keeper.

Queen Vashti was more than just a woman of royal status she was a woman of conviction, courage, and compassion. She understood the deep responsibility that came with being her sisters' keeper. In a time when women were often silenced and devalued, Queen Vashti stood as a beacon of dignity and strength. She knew that being your sister's keeper meant showing up in her time of need, offering strength when she feels weak, and being present so, she never has to walk through her battles alone.

To be a sister's keeper is to recognize when your sister is weary and to be the shoulder she can lean on. It's the quiet strength in the background that says, "I've got you." Queen Vashti embodied this kind of sisterhood. She didn't just stand for herself; she stood for every woman in the kingdom who had ever felt voiceless or unseen. Her refusal to be paraded before the king's guests wasn't just about personal dignity it was an act of collective courage. She carried the weight of every woman on her shoulders who watched her, hoping for someone to finally say "no" to disgrace and "yes" to self-worth.

It is deeply comforting to know that in times of trouble, we don't have to stand alone. That someone will step in

"I Was Born To Be A Queen"

when we are too weak to stand on our own. Imagine how isolating it could have been if Queen Vashti didn't have the other women to confide in, to lean on, or to draw strength from. As a leader, Queen Vashti needed the support of the women around her just as much as they needed her to be their example. Leadership is not about standing above others it's about standing *with* them.

There are times in life when unexpected trials come crashing in, when we're blindsided by pain, confusion, or injustice. In those moments, the power of sisterhood becomes a lifeline. Queen Vashti's courageous decision reminds us that we draw strength from one another. Her stand was not only for her own dignity but for the dignity of the countless women who had suffered in silence.

Being a sister's keeper means holding space for one another, covering each other in prayer, offering a listening ear, and choosing love over judgment.

Queen Vashti's example teaches us that when one woman rises, she creates space for others to rise with her. She understood that true leadership is rooted in empathy, solidarity, and love. And through her boldness, she became a powerful symbol of what it means to stand not just for yourself but for your sisters, too.

"I Was Born To Be A Queen"

Answer These Questions:

What does being your sister's keeper mean to you personally and spiritually?

Have there been moments in your life when you needed someone to stand by you and support you?

Do you believe Queen Vashti set a powerful example of what it means to be a sister's keeper?

Do you have strong, supportive women in your circle who genuinely have your back?

"I Was Born To Be A Queen"

"Uncrowned But Not Unshaken: The Legacy of Queen Vashti"

Prayer:

Lord, Help Me Be My Sister's Keeper

Lord, help me to truly understand what it means to be my sister's keeper not just in words, but in action, in love, and in presence. Teach me to carry her burdens when she is weary, to pray for her when she cannot find the words, and to stand in the gap when she feels like giving up. Let my heart be sensitive to her struggles, my ears open to her silent cries, and my spirit alert to her unspoken needs. Surround me, Lord, with a circle of strong, compassionate, and faithful women who will lift me up when I'm down and walk beside me through every season. Let us be a sisterhood that honors You by honoring one another.

In Jesus' Name, Amen.

"I Was Born To Be A Queen"

I Will Not Let Others Depreciate My Value

Here are some powerful scriptures that speak to knowing your worth and not allowing others to diminish your value:

Proverbs 31:25 (NLT)
"She is clothed with strength and dignity, and she laughs without fear of the future."

This verse reminds you that your strength and dignity come from God.

Psalm 139:14 (NIV)
"I praise you because I am fearfully and wonderfully made; your works are wonderful; I know that full well."

You are wonderfully made by God. Your value is divine and untouchable.

"I Was Born To Be A Queen"

Isaiah 43:4 (NIV)
"Since you are precious and honored in my sight, and because I love you…"

God sees you as precious and honored. Let His view define your worth not the opinions of others.

Galatians 1:10 (ESV)
"For am I now seeking the approval of man, or of God? Or am I trying to please man? If I were still trying to please man, I would not be a servant of Christ."

Your value isn't based on the approval of others, but on God's truth about who you are.

"Queen Vashti Refused to Let the King Depreciate Her Value."

Queen Vashti was a woman of strength, dignity, and unwavering self-respect. In a time when women were expected to be silent and submissive, she boldly chose to protect her worth rather than be reduced to an object of display. She was determined not to let the king or anyone else depreciate her value. Her decision to say "No" was not an act of rebellion but a declaration of dignity. She stood firm in the face of public scrutiny and royal authority because she knew her worth did not come from a crown or a title it came from within, and ultimately, from God.

"I Was Born To Be A Queen"

"Uncrowned But Not Unshaken: The Legacy of Queen Vashti"

I envision Queen Vashti as a brave and courageous woman *whose Inner Strength radiated* far beyond the walls of the palace. She didn't operate from a place of low self-esteem or fear. She wasn't hesitant or unsure of who she was. On the contrary, she was rooted in confidence and caried herself with the kind of boldness that only comes from knowing your purpose and refusing to compromise it. Her quiet yet powerful stand became a voice for every woman who has ever been made to feel small, unheard, or devalued.

So many times, as women, we allow society, relationships, or even systems to dictate what we can and cannot do. We're told to shrink, to stay in our place, to conform leaving us feeling helpless and unseen. But Queen Vashti breaks that mold. She reminds us that it is more than okay to stand up for what you believe in. She gives us permission to protect our boundaries, guard our bodies, and honor our voices. She shows us that dignity is not something we trade for comfort or status. It's something you uphold, even when it costs you everything.

Queen Vashti's story empowers us to reject anything or anyone that attempts to diminish our God-given value. Her legacy is a rallying cry for women everywhere: You are worthy. You are valuable. *You are allowed to say no.*

"I Was Born To Be A Queen"

"Uncrowned But Not Unshaken: The Legacy of Queen Vashti"

Never let anyone depreciate your worth. Like Queen Vashti, walk in boldness, clothed in strength and dignity, knowing *that when* you honor yourself, you honor God.

Answer These Questions:

Do you ever feel like you've allowed others to diminish your value or worth?

How important is it for you to confidently use your voice and speak your truth?

Do you recognize that when you walk in the power God has given you, you are bringing honor to Him?

What area of your life do you feel God is calling you to grow and mature in?

"I Was Born To Be A Queen"

Prayer:

Lord, thank You for reminding me that I must never depreciate the talents, gifts, and purpose You have so graciously placed within me. You formed me with intention, equipped me with power, and filled me with divine potential. Forgive me for the times I've doubted what You placed inside of me or allowed fear and the opinions of others to silence my voice.

In Jesus' Name, Amen.

"I Was Born To Be A Queen"

I Am Willing To Take The Risk

2 Timothy 1:7 (KJV)

"For God hath not given us the spirit of fear; but of power, and of love, and of a sound mind."

This reminds us that the courage to take risks doesn't come from within alone, but from the Spirit of God that is empowering us.

Queen Vashti: "Willing to Take the Risk for *Her* Dignity."

Queen Vashti was a woman of unshakable integrity and bold conviction. She understood that dignity is not something that can be negotiated or traded it is something you fight for. When faced with the king's humiliating command, Queen Vashti chose the path of risk over the comfort of compliance. She was willing to sacrifice her crown, her position, and her security to uphold her self-worth. That decision alone marks her as one of the most courageous women in biblical history.

"I Was Born To Be A Queen"

"Uncrowned But Not Unshaken: The Legacy of Queen Vashti"

I once heard a little Jamaican boy say, *"You must fight for what you want, because what you want will not fight for you."* This powerful truth reminds me of Queen Vashti. She fought not with weapons, or anger, or silence, but with the strength to say "No." She fought for *what was* important to her: her dignity, her self-respect, and the *example she* would leave behind for other women.

Taking a risk doesn't come easy. It requires courage, inner strength, and trust in something greater than yourself. Risk exposes who we truly are and reveals the depth of what God has placed inside us. Queen Vashti's story reminds us that the boldness to take a stand is not just a moment of bravery it is a calling. We are called to the righteousness of God. We are called to let our voices be heard, even when it's inconvenient or unpopular. We are called to walk by faith, not fear. We are called to be the example that others can follow just like Queen Vashti.

Her story teaches us that playing it safe is not always the most faithful option. Sometimes, the very thing God asks of us will come wrapped in discomfort and risk. But those who are willing to take that risk are usually the ones who rise, lead, and make a lasting difference.

Queen Vashti may have lost her crown, but she gained something far greater *a legacy of strength, courage, and unwavering dignity.* And that is a risk worth taking.

"I Was Born To Be A Queen"

Answer These Questions:

Are you willing to step out in faith and take a bold risk?

Do you consider yourself someone who embraces risk for a greater purpose?

Are you ready to fight for what truly matters to you?

Looking back, do you believe the risks you've taken were worth the outcome?

"I Was Born To Be A Queen"

"Uncrowned But Not Unshaken:
The Legacy of Queen Vashti"

Prayer:

"Lord, Thank You for Making Me a Courageous Risk Taker." Lord, I come before You with a heart full of gratitude. Thank You for showing me the importance of being a risk taker not for the sake of pride or recognition, but for the sake of purpose, truth, and righteousness. Thank You for loving me unconditionally, even when I've doubted myself or hesitated to move forward. Your love strengthens me and gives me the courage to step into the unknown, trusting that You have already gone before me.

In Jesus' Name, Amen.

"I Was Born To Be A Queen"

God Will Reward My Faithfulness

Hebrews 6:10 (NIV)

"God is not unjust; he will not forget your work and the love you have shown him as you have helped his people and continue to help them."

This verse reminds us that God sees every act of service, every sacrifice, and every moment of obedience. He honors those who remain faithful to Him and to the calling He has placed on their lives.

Galatians 6:9 (NIV)

"Let us not become weary in doing good, for at the proper time we will reap a harvest if we do not give up."

This encourages us to stay faithful, knowing that God has a reward prepared in His perfect timing.

I believe with all my heart that God will never forget our faithfulness. Every sacrifice, every stand for righteousness, every quiet act of obedience He sees it all. He is a rewarder of those who diligently seek Him (Hebrews 11:6), and

"I Was Born To Be A Queen"

He honors those who remain steadfast in their devotion, even when it's difficult. Faithfulness is never overlooked by God, and it is always rewarded in His perfect timing and divine way.

When I think about Queen Vashti, I don't see a disgraced woman whose story ended in rejection. I see a woman whose courage and dignity caught the attention of Heaven. She said no to the King's request because she chose self-respect, integrity, and honor over public humiliation. And even though that decision cost her the crown, I choose to believe that God had a greater crown waiting for her a crown not made by man but fashioned by the very hands of God.

Putting on my imagination hat, I see Queen Vashti living a life of serenity and purpose, far away from the noise of the palace and the judgment of men. I see her dwelling in a beautiful place of peace, crowned not by position, but by divine favor. In my heart, she remains the regal olive-skinned queen, full of grace, strength, and unwavering resolve. The King may have stripped her of a title, but God never stripped her of her worth.

This vision isn't just for Queen Vashti it's for us. In this world where doing the right thing is often costly, where standing for truth can feel lonely, and where faithfulness can feel unrewarded, let us not grow weary. Let us stay

"I Was Born To Be A Queen"

faithful to what God has called us to do. Even when we can't see the fruit right away, we must believe that our faithfulness is planting seeds for a harvest that will come.

God will never give up on us. He is always faithful, even when we falter. Our lives are safely tucked in the palm of His mighty hand, and there is no greater place to be than in the hands of our loving Father. So, keep showing up. Keep standing strong. Keep saying "yes" to God and "no" to compromise. For the same God who saw Queen Vashti's courage sees yours and He will reward your faithfulness in due time.

Answer These Questions:

Do you understand that God will never give up on you, no matter what?

When you reflect on Queen Vashti's story, what comes to your heart and mind?

"I Was Born To Be A Queen"

"Uncrowned But Not Unshaken: The Legacy of Queen Vashti"

Are you aware that choosing to do what is right often comes with a cost?

Do you believe that your faithfulness never goes unnoticed by God?

Prayer:

Lord, I come before You with a heart full of gratitude. Thank You for being a God who honors faithfulness. Even when others may not see the sacrifices I've made or the steps, I've taken in obedience to You, I know that nothing goes unnoticed by You. You are the rewarder of those who diligently seek You, and I trust that every act of faith, every moment of endurance, and every decision to follow You will bear fruit in Your perfect timing.

In Jesus' Name, Amen.

"I Was Born To Be A Queen"

I Will Seek Godly Advice

James 1:5 (NIV)
"If any of you lacks wisdom, you should ask God, who gives generously to all without finding fault, and it will be given to you."

The foundation of godly counsel starts by asking *God* for wisdom first.

"Detailed Description: Seeking Godly Counsel and the Power of a Trusted Circle."

I also believe that God deeply desires for us to seek *Godly counsel* wisdom and advice from individuals who genuinely fear the Lord, walk in integrity, and stand righteously before Him. These are not just good people; they are God-fearing individuals who are led by the Spirit and rooted in truth. They are the kind of people who don't just tell us what we *want* to hear, but what we *need* to hear, lovingly pointing us back to the Word of God.

"I Was Born To Be A Queen"

Scripture makes it clear in **Matthew 6:33**: *"But seek first the kingdom of God and His righteousness, and all these things will be added to you."* This directive reminds us that before we seek answers from the world, our first pursuit must be to align ourselves with the will of God and often, God will speak to us through the wise counsel of those He has placed around us.

Protecting our inner circle is not just wise it's essential. Not everyone is qualified to speak into your life, and not everyone has the spiritual maturity or discernment to guide you in righteousness. That's why we must ask God to send us the *right* people those who will love us, pray for us, correct us when we're wrong, and encourage us when we're weary. It's not always easy to open up and expose our weaknesses, but when you're surrounded by the right people who carry God's heart it becomes easier to be vulnerable, to heal, and to grow.

Let's be honest: it takes humility to admit our flaws and allow our hearts to be open to the truth. But Scripture reminds us in **Romans 3:23**, *"For all have sinned and fall short of the glory of God."* None of us are perfect. The flesh is weak, but the Spirit of the Lord is strong, and God often strengthens us through the wisdom, support, and accountability of godly friends.

"I Was Born To Be A Queen"

I imagine Queen Vashti, in her time of decision, had a circle of women or trusted individuals who gave her sound advice those who supported her in taking a stand for her dignity, even in the face of loss. Like her, we all need people who will stand with us, pray with us, and guide us toward what is just, holy, and pleasing to God.

In closing, seeking Godly counsel is not a sign of weakness; it's a sign of wisdom. It reflects a heart that is submitted to God and open to correction, guidance, and truth. When we surround ourselves with people who fear the Lord, we are building a foundation of strength, truth, and protection for our lives and that is a blessing we cannot afford to live without.

Answer These Questions:

Who are the Godly individuals you turn to for wise and spiritual counsel?

Have you asked God for guidance in choosing the right people to be in your trusted spiritual circle?

"I Was Born To Be A Queen"

Do you feel safe and comfortable opening your heart to those trusted Godly voices in your life?

What is holding you back from forming your trusted circle could it be fear, shame, or past hurt?

Prayer:

Lord, help me to seek Your advice on choosing my trusted godly circle. I don't want to be surrounded by just anyone I want to be surrounded by those who reflect Your heart, walk in Your truth and seek Your will above all else. Give me spiritual discernment to recognize the people, You've assigned to walk with me in this season of my life those who are rooted in righteousness, guided by Your Word filled with Your Spirit.

In Jesus' Name, Amen.

"I Was Born To Be A Queen"

I Am Willing To Be A Part Of The Master Plan

Isaiah 6:8 (NIV)

"Then I heard the voice of the Lord saying, 'Whom shall I send? And who will go for us?' And I said, 'Here am I. Send me!'"

This verse captures a spirit of willingness, obedience, and surrender to God's divine plan. Like the prophet Isaiah, you are saying, *"Lord, I'm available. Use me for Your purpose. I want to be a part of what You are doing."*

Willing to Be a Part of the Master Plan: A Reflection on Queen Vashti and Isaiah 6:8

This scripture speaks so loudly to the spirit and strength of Queen Vashti. Though her name is often overlooked or dismissed, I believe she was a woman prepared by God, positioned by Him, and willing to be a part of His divine master plan. Her story may appear to be one of loss on the surface, but beneath it lies the foundation of a powerful divine setup.

"I Was Born To Be A Queen"

"Uncrowned But Not Unshaken: The Legacy of Queen Vashti"

Queen Vashti was not merely a woman who said *no* to the king she was a woman who said yes to God. Her decision to stand up for her dignity, her worth, and her values was not random; it was guided by a higher calling. I truly believe that she surrendered to the unseen will of God, even if she didn't fully understand the outcome. That is faith in action. That is Isaiah 6:8 in motion "Here am I use me"

Her boldness set the tone for the arrival of Queen Esther. Let us pause for a moment and imagine *What if Queen Vashti had bowed to the pressure? What if she had remained silent and allowed herself to be publicly disgraced?* There may have been no Esther to rise up "for such a time as this" (Esther 4:14), and the legacy of the Jewish people could have been wiped out. But because God had a greater plan, He used Queen Vashti as the courageous forerunner to shift the atmosphere, to make space for destiny, and to declare that women have a voice, purpose, and a divine assignment.

That's how our God operates. Jeremiah 29:11 reminds us that He knows the plans He has for us plans to prosper us, not to harm us; plans to give us a hope and a future. Queen Vashti's exit was not her end it was a divine beginning.

Personally, I had to learn to trust God in everything I do and everything I need to do. Life is full of distractions.

"I Was Born To Be A Queen"

"Uncrowned But Not Unshaken:
The Legacy of Queen Vashti"

The world pulls us in different directions, demanding our attention, cluttering our minds, and making it easy to forget our divine purpose. If we are not careful, we'll find ourselves entangled in the noise and not attuned to the voice of God.

That's why Queen Vashti's story is so powerful. She was clear on what she needed to do. She did not allow fear, public opinion, or pressure to detour her. She did not allow distractions to drown out her inner conviction. She stood in her quiet strength and made a decision that aligned with the master plan of God even if the world didn't understand.

Now, I ask you:

What are *you* doing to stay on the right track?

Are you surrendered to God's plan for your life?

Are you willing to let go of comfort and take hold of purpose?

Can you boldly say like Isaiah, *"Here am I. Send me"?*

Let Queen Vashti's story reminds you that obedience to God is never in vain. Even if it costs you something, even

"I Was Born To Be A Queen"

if it removes you from one place to another, it positions you for something far greater in His Kingdom.

I want you to stay focused, faithful, and stay willing.

Answer These Questions:

Are you willing to surrender and take your place in God's master plan for your life?

What inspires you most about Queen Vashti's story and the stand she took?

What purpose or calling do you believe God is leading you to fulfill?

"I Was Born To Be A Queen"

"Uncrowned But Not Unshaken: The Legacy of Queen Vashti"

Are you fully trusting God to lead and guide you in every area of your life?

Prayer:

Heavenly Father,

I come before You with a heart that longs to walk in step with Your divine will. Lord, help me to see Your master plan for my life the plan that You designed before I ever took my first breath. I know that Your thoughts are higher than mine and Your ways are greater than anything I could ever imagine. Let me not become distracted by temporary pleasures or the applause of man but help me to fix my eyes on You the Author and Finisher of my faith.

In Jesus' Name, Amen.

"I Was Born To Be A Queen"

I Was Born To Be A Queen

Psalm 139:14 (NIV)

"I praise you because I am fearfully and wonderfully made; your works are wonderful; I know that full well."

This scripture reminds you that you were handcrafted by God with purpose, beauty, and intention. Being "fearfully and wonderfully made" means you were born with divine excellence you were created to walk in dignity, strength, and grace. That's what Queens are made of.

You weren't just born to exist you were born to reign in your God-given identity.

1 Peter 2:9 (NKJV)

"But you are a chosen generation, a royal priesthood, a holy nation, His own special people, that you may proclaim the praises of Him who called you out of darkness into His marvelous light."

This verse reminds you that you were born with worth, dignity, and a God-given crown. You are a Queen because your Father is the King of Kings.

"I Was Born To Be A Queen"

I Was Born to Be a Queen – A Reflection on Queen Vashti

I am totally convinced that Queen Vashti was *destined* to be a Queen. Her position was not accidental, and her courage was not random. She was chosen for a divine assignment. Psalm 139:14 echoes this truth so clearly: *"I praise you because I am fearfully and wonderfully made; your works are wonderful; I know that full well."* This scripture is a reminder that everything God creates is intentional, powerful, and filled with purpose including you and me.

Too often in life, we forget who we are and more importantly, who's we are. We let others' voices define us. Remember, these are voices that didn't create us and didn't call us into our greatness. They cannot shape our identity. We've been told that we're not good enough, not strong enough, not worthy of love, respect, or leadership. But those are all lies of the enemy.

God only creates greatness. When He formed us in our mother's womb, He did so with royalty in mind. He wove purpose, dignity, and power into every fiber of our being. Greatness is knitted into our very DNA.

I have chosen to reject the lies of the enemy and embrace the truth of my identity in Christ. I choose to believe in my *greatness* not because of who I am on my own, but because of *who God says I am*. I am fearfully and wonderfully made. I am divinely appointed. I was born to be a Queen.

I believe Queen Vashti knew this about herself. She carried the confidence of a woman who understood her worth. That's why she found it *easy to say no* to the king's command because she refused to be dishonored, degraded, or reduced to an object. She knew she was more than a crown, more than a title she was God's creation, full of dignity, strength, and value.

Queen Vashti's story teaches us that when you know who you are, you don't have to settle for less. You don't bow to culture or compromise your values to keep a position. You walk in truth. You walk in courage. And sometimes, you walk away in obedience to the One who created you.

Like Queen Vashti, I now know I was born to be a Queen. And so were you.

Answer These Questions:

Have you embraced the truth that you were created to walk in the royalty of a Queen?

"I Was Born To Be A Queen"

"Uncrowned But Not Unshaken: The Legacy of Queen Vashti"

Do you have the boldness to stand firm and say "no" when necessary?

Do you truly believe in the greatness God has planted within you?

Have you unknowingly accepted the false labels others have spoken over your life?

Prayer:

Lord, help me to remember that You created in me a Queen and that I have been destined to do great things. When others speak negativity over me, remind me that I am fearfully and wonderfully made by You and that there is absolutely nothing I cannot do with You on my side.

In Jesus' Name, Amen.

"I Was Born To Be A Queen"

I Am A God Pleaser Not a People Pleaser

Galatians 1:10 (NIV)

"Am I now trying to win the approval of human beings, or of God? Or am I trying to please people? If I were still trying to please people, I would not be a servant of Christ."

Explanation:

This verse clearly reminds us that our primary focus should be on seeking God's approval, not the validation or acceptance of others. When we live to please people, we often compromise our values, dim our light, or silence our truth. But when we choose to live as servants of Christ, we are called to honor Him above all else even when it isn't popular or easy.

Let this verse be your anchor when you're tempted to conform to others' expectations. Remember: You were created to glorify God, not to fit into man's mold.

"I Was Born To Be A Queen"

"Don't Be a People Pleaser – Be a God Pleaser: A Lesson from Queen Vashti"

One of the most admirable qualities about Queen Vashti is that she was not a people pleaser she was a God pleaser. Her actions in the book of Esther are a bold and timeless reminder that we were never created to fit into man's mold, but to glorify God in all that we do. Her refusal to obey the King's degrading request wasn't an act of rebel lion it was an act of reverence. Reverence for herself. Reverence for the sacredness of her body. Reverence for the God who created her in His image.

Let this truth anchor your soul: You were created to glorify God, not to gain the approval of people. In a world that constantly pressures women to conform, to expose, to compete for attention by compromising their dignity, Queen Vashti stands out as a radiant example of godly strength and self-worth. She was not swayed by the opinions of the king's nobles, nor was she intimidated by the potential consequences of her decision. Her worth was not determined by applause or acceptance her worth was anchored in something eternal.

Today, we as women must reclaim that same courage. We must rise above the cultural trends that tell us we need to show more skin, speak less truth, or dim our light to be accepted. When we wear clothing that reveals our bodies

"I Was Born To Be A Queen"

in ways that invite lust rather than respect, we must ask ourselves: *What am I really communicating? Who am I really trying to please?* if the answer is anything other than God, we've lost sight of who we truly are.

Our bodies are temples of the Holy Spirit. They are sacred, beautifully made by God to be honored not put on display to gain the fleeting approval of man. Just as Queen Vashti chose dignity over disgrace, we must choose modesty over manipulation, purpose over popularity, and God's approval over public opinion.

The world will always try to dictate who we should be, how we should look, and what we should tolerate. But we must be women who know our value, who walk in wisdom, and who carry ourselves in a way that says: *"I belong to God."*

So, take courage from Queen Vashti's story. Her refusal to be a people pleaser set the stage for divine purpose to unfold.

Don't be a people pleaser. Be a God pleaser. Your worth is not up for negotiation.

"I Was Born To Be A Queen"

Answer These Questions:

Are you living for the approval of people or the approval of God?

Have you recognized that your worth is non-negotiable and God-defined?

What message do you believe a woman sends when she chooses to dress without modesty?

Do you see how the world constantly tries to define your identity and worth?

Prayer:

Lord, today I come before You with a sincere heart, asking for Your strength and guidance. Help me not to be a people pleaser, swayed by the opinions, expectations, or

"I Was Born To Be A Queen"

approval of others. Let my heart seek only Your pleasure and Your will. Teach me what it means to walk in true obedience to You even when it means standing alone.

In Jesus' Name, Amen

I Will Stand Firm On My Decision

1 Corinthians 15:58 (NIV)

"Therefore, my dear brothers and sisters, stand firm. Let nothing move you. Always give yourselves fully to the work of the Lord, because you know that your labor in the Lord is not in vain."

This verse encourages us to remain unwavering in our decisions when they are aligned with God's will. Like Queen Vashti, we are called to stand firm even when it's not popular because God honors bold obedience.

Stand Firm on Your Decisions

It is critically important to stand firm on the decisions you make especially when those decisions are rooted in righteousness, dignity, and obedience to God. In a world filled with noise, pressure, and distractions, it can be tempting to second-guess yourself or give in to the opinions of others. But you must remain grounded in your convictions. When you know in your heart what is right, do not allow anyone or anything to sway you from that path that God has for you.

"I Was Born To Be A Queen"

"Uncrowned But Not Unshaken: The Legacy of Queen Vashti"

Queen Vashti is a powerful example of this kind of unwavering strength. She made a courageous decision to honor her self-worth and refused to be treated as an object, even though it meant facing rejection from the king. Remember her boldness wasn't rebellion it was righteousness. She stood firm, not because it was easy, but because it was right. She wasn't persuaded by the pressure of the court, the expectations of society, or the fear of consequence. Her stand teaches us the value of inner strength, self-respect, and faith in a greater purpose.

As followers of Christ, we are also called to stand firm in our faith, firm in our values, firm in our identity. The love we have for our Lord and Savior Jesus Christ should anchor every decision we make. And when the world tries to pull us in another direction, we must choose to remain steadfast in the truth of God's Word.

Standing firm will not always be popular. Sometimes it will cost you friends, opportunities, or acceptance. But the reward is far greater peace with God, a clear conscience, and the honor of walking in His will. 1 Corinthians 15:58 reminds us, *"Stand firm. Let nothing move you."* That means no matter how loud the world gets, how intense the pressure becomes, or how lonely the road may feel, we must remain faithful to God. We don't compromise. We don't shrink back. We don't let others' opinions define us.

"I Was Born To Be A Queen"

Let your decisions reflect your love and reverence for God. Be confident in your yes and your no. And when you make a stand for what is right, hold your ground. You are not alone God is with you, and He will strengthen you every step of the way.

Stand firm. Be unshaken. Be faithful. God honors those who honor Him.

Answer These Questions:

Are you willing to stand firm in your decisions, even when they carry life-changing consequences?

How do you respond when you feel yourself being drawn away from the path God has set for you?

Are you prepared to lose friends for the sake of doing what is right in God's eyes?

"I Was Born To Be A Queen"

Is Christ the steady anchor that holds your life in place through every storm?

Prayer:

Lord, I come before You with a heart that desires to remain rooted in Your truth. In a world full of distractions, temptations, and shifting values, help me to stand firm on Your Word. Let Your promises be the foundation upon which I build my life. Remind me daily that You are my rock unshakable, immovable, and constant in all Your ways.

In Jesus' Name, Amen.

I will not be afraid to walk in my courage

Joshua 1:9 (NIV)
"Have I not commanded you? Be strong and courageous. Do not be afraid; do not be discouraged, for the Lord your God will be with you wherever you go."

This verse is a clear reminder that God has *commanded* us to walk in courage, not fear. His presence empowers us to move forward boldly, no matter the obstacles.

"Queen Vashti Was Not Afraid to Walk in Her Courage"

Queen Vashti was a bold and courageous woman who was not afraid to stand firm in her values and convictions. Her decision to say "no" to the king's degrading request wasn't just an act of defiance it was an act of *godly courage*. She walked in her power without hesitation, knowing that her dignity, self-worth, and purpose were worth more than

"I Was Born To Be A Queen"

pleasing people. Queen Vashti teaches us that walking in courage is not about being reckless; it's about knowing who you are and *whose* you are.

So many times, in life, we shrink back from our gifts because of fear, discouragement, or the opinions of others. We hesitate to walk in what God has placed inside of us. But what we must realize is that we are never alone. Just as God was with Queen Vashti, He is with us guiding, protecting and strengthening us. That divine presence gives us the courage to press forward, even when the path is uncertain.

When we walk boldly in the gifts God has given us, we are fulfilling our divine destiny. We are honoring God with our obedience and trust. Scripture reminds us that *"your gift will make room for you and bring you before great men"* (Proverbs 18:16). That means the very talents, callings, and abilities He has placed within us will open doors and lead us into places of influence and purpose.

Queen Vashti's story is not just a historical moment it is a blueprint for how to walk courageously with grace. She didn't let fear speak louder than her faith. She stood with confidence, and so can we. When we know that God is with us, we can walk boldly, speak boldly, and live bodly just like Queen Vashti.

"I Was Born To Be A Queen"

Answer These Questions:

Are you confidently walking in the boldness and courage that God has placed within you?

Who are the voices speaking into your life, and are they pushing you closer to your God-given purpose?

Are you willing to press forward in faith, even when the journey is met with obstacles and opposition?

What gifts has God entrusted to you and are you using them faithfully to live out your divine calling?

Prayer:

Lord, help me to walk in my courage the kind of courage that comes from knowing You are with me. Teach me not to shrink back in fear, but to move forward in boldness

"I Was Born To Be A Queen"

and strength. Remove every ounce of doubt, insecurity, and hesitation that seeks to hold me back from fulfilling the purpose You have placed within me.

In Jesus' name, Amen.

"I Was Born To Be A Queen"

A Time To Walk In Faith

Hebrews 11:1 (NKJV)
"Now faith is the substance of things hoped for, the evidence of things not seen."

This verse emphasizes that faith is the foundation of our hope and trust in what God has promised, even when we can't yet see it. It's a clear call to walk boldly in faith, trusting Him beyond what is visible.

2 Corinthians 5:7 (NIV)
"For we live by faith, not by sight."

This verse reminds us of, that walking in faith means trusting God's plan even when we can't see the outcome. It's about moving forward with confidence, knowing He is guiding every step.

I believe that Queen Vashti recognized that this was her moment to walk boldly in faith a crucial turning point not just in her own life, but in the lives of countless women in the kingdom.

"I Was Born To Be A Queen"

"Uncrowned But Not Unshaken: The Legacy of Queen Vashti"

She understood that her decision carried weight, not only as a personal stand but as a powerful example for others to follow. Sometimes, God calls us to a higher purpose one that stretches us far beyond what we can see or fully comprehend. For Queen Vashti, this was one of those divine moments.

She knew there would be consequences for her choice to refuse the king's command, yet she was willing to face them all. Those consequences meant far less to her than compromising her integrity, her dignity, and her calling. Her obedience to what was right in the sight of God and in the mirror of her own soul was far more valuable than the temporary favor of man.

The essence of faith is trusting God when there is no visible evidence, and Queen Vashti demonstrated that truth. Hebrews 11:1 reminds us that *"faith is the substance of things hoped for, the evidence of things not seen."* Though the future was uncertain, Queen Vashti made up her mind to do what was right and leave the results in God's hands.

She chose to walk by faith, not fear by conviction, not convenience. And that is the kind of faith we are all called to. True faith means moving forward with courage and confidence, even when the outcome is unclear, trusting that God is in control of it all. Like Queen Vashti, we must

"I Was Born To Be A Queen"

be willing to take bold steps, knowing that faith is not about what we can see it's about who we trust.

Answer These Questions:

Do you find it difficult at times to fully walk by faith?

When you're called to walk by faith, are you willing to surrender the outcome to God?

What emotions rise up in you when you're walking by faith through uncertain circumstances?

Have you come to understand that walking by faith requires bold conviction, not the comfort of convenience or the grip of fear?

"I Was Born To Be A Queen"

Prayer:

Lord, help me to understand the true importance of walking by faith. Teach me not to rely on what my natural eyes see, but to trust fully in Your divine power and perfect plan. Strengthen my heart to believe that even when the evidence is not yet visible, You are working behind the scenes for my good. Remind me, Lord, that my present circumstances do not define my future Your promises do.

In Jesus' name Amen

God Will Close One Door to Open a Bigger One

Revelation 3:7-8 (NIV):
"What he opens no one can shut, and what he shuts no one can open. I know your deeds. See, I have placed before you an open door that no one can shut."

This passage reminds us that God is in full control. When He closes one opportunity, it's not the end—it's His way of guiding us to something greater that no one can take away.

Sometimes, we become so settled in where we are that we don't even realize we've stopped growing. Comfort becomes our normal, and in that space, we often lose the hunger for what's next. But God never intended for us to live a stagnant life. He created us for movement, transformation, and elevation. That's why He will often close a door not to punish us, but to prepare us for something greater.

We may not always understand it in the moment. The closed door may feel like rejection, betrayal, or even failure. The truth is it is a redirection. God sees what we can't see. He knows when the season has ended, even if we're still trying to make it work. And because He loves us too much He will not let us settle for less than what He created us for, He sends a divine disturbance like a *volcano* to erupt our carefully constructed comfort zones.

That volcano may come in the form of a job loss, a relationship ending, a shift in location, or a spiritual awakening. It shakes the very ground we stand on, forcing us to move, to re-evaluate, to grow, and most importantly, to trust Him. It is not meant to destroy us but to shift us into position for the new door He is preparing to open a door that leads to a bigger opportunity, a greater purpose, and a deeper level of destiny.

God is not done with you. He is simply repositioning you for the *next level of greatness* He has planned for your life. Don't mourn the closed door too long. Don't fight the eruption. Embrace the shift, because what's coming is far better than what's behind you.

So, I'm going to take a moment and use my imagination to envision what may have become of Queen Vashti's life after she courageously chose to stand for her dignity. I truly believe that God, in His sovereignty, closed one door but only to open a greater one. Though the crown was taken from her by earthly hands, I imagine that God

"I Was Born To Be A Queen"

placed upon her head a different kind of crown one of honor, purpose, and peace.

I believe that God was not finished with her story. Her "No" to the king was not the end, but a divine redirection toward something far more meaningful. In my heart, I see Queen Vashti walking into a new season filled with love that honored herself worth, friendships that celebrated her values, and a peaceful life surrounded by those who respected her boldness and integrity.

I imagine her living in a quiet, beautiful place perhaps tucked away in a tranquil garden dwelling where the sounds of rushing waters and rustling trees became her new throne room. Instead of being remembered as a banished queen, I see her as a chosen vessel used by God to pave the way for greater things. Her strength became her legacy. Her stand created a path for Queen Esther. And even though history tried to silence her, Heaven celebrated her.

In this version of her story, I believe that God gave her double for her trouble healing for the pain, restoration for the rejection, and joy for the sorrow. Because when we choose to do what is right in the eyes of God, even when the world calls it rebellion, God calls it obedience. I believe Queen Vashti walked into a destiny that the world couldn't see a future full of God's peace, wrapped in divine

"I Was Born To Be A Queen"

favor, and overflowing with a love that only God could provide.

Answer These Questions:

If you allowed your imagination to take flight, how would you envision the next chapter of Queen Vashti's life unfolding?

Have you ever considered that God had more in store for Queen Vashti that her story didn't end with the loss of her crown?

Do you trust that when God closes a door, He's preparing to open one far greater than you could imagine?

Can you see that when you choose to embrace life's divine shifts, you position yourself to receive something far better than what you left behind?

"I Was Born To Be A Queen"

"Uncrowned But Not Unshaken: The Legacy of Queen Vashti"

Prayer:

Heavenly Father,

Thank You for the gift of vision and for allowing me to catch a glimpse of the beautiful future You have prepared for me. Even when my present feels uncertain, I choose to trust in Your promises and plans. Lord, I surrender everything that may be holding me back the doubts, the fears, the pain of past disappointments, and the attachments to what no longer serves Your purpose in my life.

In Jesus' name, Amen.

"I Was Born To Be A Queen"

I have Created You For A Different Purpose

Jeremiah 1:5 (NIV)
"Before I formed you in the womb I knew you, before you were born, I set you apart; I appointed you as a prophet to the nations."

This verse speaks directly to God's intentional design and unique purpose for each of us. It reminds us that we were not created by accident we were set apart for a divine and different purpose even before we were born.

"Before Queen Vashti was born, God had a purpose and plan for her life."

Let us step into the realm of divine imagination and spiritual reflection let us put on our *imagination hat* and travel back to the early days of Queen Vashti's life, long before she wore a crown or sat on a throne.

I believe that Queen Vashti was born into royalty, not just by human lineage but by divine assignment. From the

"I Was Born To Be A Queen"

very beginning, God had greatness in store for her. Her childhood was not an accident. Every detail the home she was born into, the people who influenced her, and even the culture that surrounded her was a part of God's intentional design to prepare and groom her for the purpose He had already written in the heavens for her. She was not just born to be a queen in title she was born to walk out a divine mandate.

There was a heavenly assignment on her life, a sacred calling that had been placed upon her before she took her first breath. Jeremiah 1:5 echoes this truth: *"Before I formed you in the womb I knew you, before you were born, I set you apart…"* *Queen* Vashti was set apart. She was chosen. She was marked for something different.

And like many of us who are called to walk in God's divine purpose, her journey was not easy. The preparation was often uncomfortable It may have been lonely. There were likely seasons of misunderstanding, where even those closest to her couldn't grasp what God was doing in her life. But that's the way God often works. He allows discomfort, not to punish us, but to *position* us. He allows us to walk through unfamiliar places, not to confuse us, but to *clarify* our calling.

God was preparing Queen Vashti day by day, trial by trial for the moment when she would have to stand for

"I Was Born To Be A Queen"

something greater than herself. He was grooming her for the moment when she would have to say **"No"** to the demands of man and **"Yes"** to her divine dignity. That kind of strength doesn't happen overnight. That kind of courage is cultivated in private before it's displayed in public.

And here's the beautiful truth: on the other side of that assignment, there was greatness waiting for her. Though she was removed from the palace, I believe she was elevated in purpose. Though the crown may have been taken from her head God placed a greater crown of honor and righteousness upon her spirit. He opened a new door that human eyes couldn't see, because what He had planned for her was beyond her imagination.

Many people looking from the outside may have misjudged her. They didn't understand her decision. They couldn't see the God ordained courage it took to refuse to be devalued. But that's because God created her for a different purpose. And often times, those who are created for something different will not be understood by those around them.

But that's okay.

Because God was doing a New Thing in her just as He is doing a New Thing in you. He was using her life as a

"I Was Born To Be A Queen"

divine example of obedience, dignity, strength, and purpose. Queen Vashti's story teaches us that we may be called to stand in uncomfortable places for a higher cause. But if we trust God's process, we will come to understand that what lies beyond our obedience is far greater than what we had to leave behind.

So, as you reflect on Queen Vashti, remember this:

You were created for a different purpose too.

And just like Queen Vashti, your story is still being written by the hand of a God who makes no mistakes. I saw a quote that I love that says God is still writing your story! Stop trying to steal the pen. In essence this statement says let God be in control.

Answer These Questions:

Have you realized that God created you for a unique and greater purpose?

Are you willing to endure the difficult seasons in order to step fully into that purpose?

"I Was Born To Be A Queen"

"Uncrowned But Not Unshaken: The Legacy of Queen Vashti"

Do you understand that your life was designed to align with divine purpose?

Are you ready to walk boldly in the purpose God has destined for you to fulfill?

Prayer:

Heavenly Father,

I come before You today with a heart that longs to walk in alignment with Your will. Lord, help me to stay focused on the plans You have already laid out for my life, even when I don't fully understand them. When the road becomes unclear, and the path feels heavy, remind me that Your ways are higher than mine and that Your purpose is always greater than what I can see in the moment.

In Jesus' name, Amen

"I Was Born To Be A Queen"

Notes

"Uncrowned But Not Unshaken:
The Legacy of Queen Vashti"

Notes

"I Was Born To Be A Queen"

Notes

Notes

Notes

Notes

Notes

Dr. Nora Believes that "Great things happen when people have Great Expectations!"

Stay in touch with Dr. Nora Shariff-Borden and Business Women On The Move For God by following along at:
Instagram @bwotmfg
Facebook @BusinessWomenontheMoveforGod
YouTube @NoraShariff3505
You can also visit https://www.bwotmfg.com/
Spiritualtouchtv.com

Dr. Nora Shariff-Borden
Founder and CEO of BWOTMFG
Stone Mountain, GA
info@bwotmfg.com

www.ingramcontent.com/pod-product-compliance
Lightning Source LLC
Chambersburg PA
CBHW051525120626
46551CB00012B/1088